Sequel to *Women are Spiritual BRIDGES*

Dancing through the Storms

A Woman's Guide to Recognizing Abuse and Weeding Out Destructive Relationships

BREN GANDY-WILSON

WestBow
PRESS
A DIVISION OF THOMAS NELSON

Cover photo by www.SweetDreamsStudios.com

Author Credits to Women are Spiritual BRIDGES and Who's To Say Cats Don't Praise!

WestBow Press books may be ordered through booksellers or by contacting:

WestBow Press
A Division of Thomas Nelson
1663 Liberty Drive
Bloomington, IN 47403
www.westbowpress.com
1-(866) 928-1240

ISBN: 978-1-4908-0682-2 (sc)
ISBN: 978-1-4908-0683-9 (e)

Library of Congress Control Number: 2013915813

Printed in the United States of America.

WestBow Press rev. date: 9/10/2013

TABLE OF CONTENTS

"By Wisdom a house is built, and through understanding it is established; through knowledge its rooms are filled with rare and beautiful treasures." **Proverbs 24:3-4**

DEDICATION

"Teach us to number our days that we may gain a heart of wisdom." Psalm 90:12

Dedicated to the up building of the Kingdom of God, one family at a time.

INTRODUCTION

The ability of men and women to live together in peace and harmony has been widely debated ever since God presented the first woman Eve to the First man Adam. Since the Fall, men and women have been busy fulfilling the prime directive given by God to be fruitful and multiply, but unfortunately, the fruit produced is not what God meant. The gap between men and women has gotten so wide and the hostilities so ugly that it is not hard to see that things have gone terribly wrong. For the sake of our children and their future, we need to get it together.

For a child, the healthy family should operate like a small nucleus of the womb it was birthed from. The family should provide all the nourishment, protection and knowledge children need to enter the world and become productive adults and giving members of society.

Some try to blame the present crisis of the family on the economy, but if you look to the past, families seem to have weathered the darkest days of depression eras, persecution and scandals by pulling together. Throughout history, individual members found their security and identities in their families. The rougher things became, the more the family pulled together. Runaway members and those in rebellions because they didn't like themselves - or they didn't like something that happened in the family, would look back to their bloodline when they came to the end of themselves. Something innate would come alive as they sifted through the thorns to reclaim the love and patience of family.

"A Charge to Keep I have…a God to Glorify
A never-dying soul to save and fit it for the sky." Charles Wesley

In the past, women saw their roles in the family as a mission, a service to God and a contribution to humanity. Love was an action word. Wives and Mothers prayed for their families and left the final results to God. Their ever present motto was "Love one another as I have loved you." (John 13:34) Mothers understood the family unit as a uniquely created nucleus of God through the union of a Woman and a Man. She saw the weaknesses of her spouse and her children and deliberately chose to cover them by showing them the God in her and extending to each the same Grace and Mercy that God had shown her. What happened to that unconditional love?

I remember going to a spiritual seminar some years ago in which the speaker said he never thought he would live to see mothers abandon their children in the great numbers he is witnessing today. He blamed it on the drug culture. He expected it from men because he had witnessed any excuse to abandon not only their children but their wives at the drop of a hat from men. I do not disagree. But I believe his diagnoses did not reach deep enough. I see drug use as a symptom, but not the root of the problem.

The answer to what happened to that unconditional love is found in the fact that most unions are not built on a strong foundation of love first for Christ and self as qualifiers to love another. Through accepting Christ as LORD and Master, we gain the keys to the Kingdom of God. Wisdom to Navigate through the storms of life is the hallmark of these keys.

Having God's wisdom within will cause us to stand still, remember who we are, consult Him, be quiet and listen for His still small voice for directions. Wisdom will cause us to see through the toughness of hurting people and the slyness of pretenders. Wisdom will cause us to go around or stay away from harmful situations. She will cause us to be ever vigilant, to watch over, pray and not faint in the midst of the storm. Wisdom will cause us to humble ourselves before Almighty God and think of the greater good rather than just about ourselves.

"I am sending you out like sheep among wolves. Therefore be as shrewd as snakes and as innocent as doves." Matthew 10:16

Dancing through the Storms is written to sound the alarm and warn women about the dangers of drifting into intimate relationships that do not have their best interest at heart.

This guide stresses using godly discernment in any relationships we form to prevent becoming a victim. Through using wisdom, women will begin to see other ways in which they might be (or might become), a victim because abuse can occur in other relationships besides the marriage covenant. It could occur on the job, in the family, with close friends and even in the church.

Each of us is the product of a complex web of systems. Some persons have suffered abusive behavior since childhood and may not recognize that they are being abused. Abuse for them, seems like "normal" behavior. Critical issues are explored in *Dancing through the Storms* which will heighten awareness of some common behavior traits (and to some subtle nuances) of abuse, whether it is verbal, mental, psychological, emotional, physical or sexual in nature.

This book is written to help recognize when behavior is not normal. After reading, the keen observer will be able to spot abusive behavior; and make wise choices about whether to try to deflect the behavior of a perpetrator or get out of the relationship. It is also written to empower victims to make decisions to survive and recover from abusive behavior. *"For God has not given us the spirit of fear; but of power, and of love, and a sound mind."* 2 Timothy 1:7

In Chapter I, *the Importance of Being Intentional*, the emphasis is on the results of wandering into unsatisfying or toxic relationships. The definition of domestic abuse is given.

In Chapter II, *What God Meant*, the reader is led to examine the effects of the fall on male and female relationships. The results of the fall left men with a need to dominate and women with a loss of identity in Christ; and therefore, the potential for domestic abuse entered in. In warping and distorting humanity, the fall has had a disastrous impact not only on how men and women relate to one another but also on all institutions and values of society. The conclusion is that we should reject the subordination of women to men and embrace God's original purpose for man and woman.

In Chapter III, *A house is not a home*, three broad types of relationship lifestyles between men and women are explored and the consequences inherent in each. These relationships are called Communal, Parasitic and Decadent. While human beings have a need to mate for love, companionship and to procreate for survival, the results of the fall of man caused these needs to become perverted. Human symbiosis is a process, and with In breeding, a cyclical one.

In Chapter IV, *Journey towards Becoming Connected*, the reader is taken through the process of humanity's birth and discovery of self, God, community and finally their lifetime companion. The reader explores the fact that there are countless attachments in the world. Every attachment brings with it responsibilities to be discerning. The first and most important attachment is to God. In God's plan for our lives, God-ordained attachments will put one in a position to ask God for what is needed or wanted and confidently expect that He will answer (John 15:7).

In Chapter V, *Releasing the Anointing to Become a Force for God*, the reader gains understanding of How God's Authority Works. There are benefits to heeding our inward witness that allow us to navigate safely through and enjoy the abundant life. You can gain godly wisdom only through making Jesus Christ LORD and Savior. "For the LORD gives wisdom, and from His mouth comes knowledge and understanding." Proverbs 2:6"

Chapter VI, *Effects of Personal Reasoning on Relationships*, the reader is admonished to examine their early childhood rearing influences when it comes to men, marriage and family; and to understand that transformation must occur in the marriage relationship. Such issues as whether romantic love is enough to sustain a relationship; role dominance and the effects of familiarity are discussed.

In Chapter VII, *Dating and Marriage God's Way*, the reader is led to analyze whether God is a match maker. What is the marriage covenant? What are the implications of making covenant vows? What is meant by evenly yoked? What does it mean to be a helper? And what makes you that special helper?

In Chapter VIII, *Does Intimacy Equal Infidelity*, four case studies are explored with specific questions after each case. The reader is asked to analyze the effects of forming close liaisons with members of the opposite sex outside of one's marriage.

In Chapter IX, *Relationship Dynamics: Distinguishing Abuse from True Love*, Countless life situational issues, from accountability to trust, is examined. The Law of attraction is analyzed and the critical reader is led to distinguish whether each situation should be interpreted as true love or as victimization.

Chapter X, *Dancing Through the Storms: Learning to Live Confidently in a Chaotic World*, the reader is encouraged to be led by the Holy Spirit, using the fruit of the Spirit which is love, joy, peace, patience, kindness, goodness, faithfulness, gentleness, self-control; as well as fasting and prayer to be empowered to correctly respond in situations that otherwise, the wrong response might lead to provoking trouble.

In Chapter XI, *Pathways to Recovery: Finding Rest and Renewal*, the reader receives encouragement thru Devotions and Prayer to aid healing and healthy reorientation to God and self.

In Chapter XII, Relationship Quiz, the reader is asked a series of questions to help them define toxic relationship dynamics. Could you be in a toxic relationship and not even know it? This quiz is only intended to give you a "flavor" about the relationship you are in. The conclusions are self directed.

The overriding principles to be understood by the end of this book are:
1) How to recognize and resist abuse in relationships;

2) Love can only be expressed properly through knowing God intimately and knowing self;

3) A healthy relationship doesn't just happen. It is the fruit resulting from heeding the promptings of the Holy Spirit and applying God's Word in every situation;

4) Marriage is a "God thing," created by God before sin entered the world;

5) A blessed marriage is a synthesis of three not two because Christ is to be the Head; and

6) Through Christ, you can fully recover from an abusive situation.

If a woman can get insight into the facts in these chapters, it will save her a lot of heartache and pain as she journeys through life. When and if she encounters the issues discussed in this book, she can engage those destructive forces in such a way that she is left whole. Spotting perpetrators of abuse through the glamour and smooth love language is difficult. After reading *Dancing through the Storms,* a woman will be in a position to side step many of the issues illustrated and recognize when it is genuine caring and when she should do more than raise an eyebrow.

Purpose

"…The aged women likewise, that they be in behavior as becomes holiness, not false accusers, not given to much wine, teachers of good things; That they may teach the young women to be sober, to love their husbands, to love their children, To be discreet, chaste, keepers at home, good, obedient to their own husbands, that the word of God be not blasphemed." Titus 2:4

Why a book for women? Well, I am a woman and I can only write from that which I am familiar with and have experienced. Certainly, I want to acknowledge that I am aware that men are often victims of abuse in relationships as well. No telling how many men have fallen prey to the wiles of the Gold Digger, the Sex Siren, the Bitter Woman, the Femme Fatale, the Damsel in Distress, and the Soap Opera Couch Potato; and all the baggage each brings into relationship. But my anointing is in the area that God has walked me through.

I cannot stress enough the gratitude I feel towards a woman of God who came into my life at my most critical need. Laura Peters became a Spiritual Bridge who led me to understand intimacy with God and pulled me back from the brink of suicide; she helped me to know my true identity and gave me hope for a marriage totally on the brink of dissolution. She did this by being faithful to her calling and by using the Word of God. She was not afraid to give her testimony and to tell me that He can do it for me too. In the first of many conversations with Laura, she asked me two questions. First, whether I was a Child of God and second if I believed God could raise a dead marriage the same way He raised Lazarus from the grave?

Laura allowed me to tell my story. It was the first step to my healing. I needed her to hear me. Getting my story out made what I was going through real because I had pretended everything was alright for so long until I had begun to believe my own deception and deny my pain.

I needed her to bear witness and validate what I was going through and that I had a right to be hurting. Laura's voice was very soothing and loving. She provided a shoulder to cry on and a listening ear. She offered hope by smiling directly into my wounded eyes and helping me envision a happier future despite my present condition. Her gaze said "You are important to God and He is grieved about what you are going through."

I was drawn to the Truth of God's Word through the way Laura provided it. Her manner and her gentle touch grasping my hands as she prayed transferred strength that let me know she had learned to weather whatever came her way through the power of God. Her own experience with loss helped her connect with me and other women she met. I was finally able to recognize myself in her. Like Laura, I want to facilitate resilience and renewal in every woman I connect with.

Therefore, in my first book, *Women are Spiritual BRIDGES*; I tell my story of how God brought me through physical, psychological, verbal and emotional abuse by bringing this Godly woman into my life. When Laura came into my life, I was not a woman of balance; in other words, I was not God centered. I didn't know who I was or how to be a wife or a mother.

Since that book is autobiographical, I began with my childhood. It might be revealed to a keen reader that as a child, my mindset and experiences while growing to adulthood predisposed me to becoming a victim of domestic abuse.

In BRIDGES, I chronicle my eventual marriage and struggles with a husband who left me four times for other women. I fall into depression as I try to raise my children, work, maintain secrecy about what was really going on in my family, as well as fight foreclosure because my husband took his paychecks with him each time he left.

Things went on like this for years until I was introduced to a woman of God. She taught me that I was breaking the first commandment by making my husband my God. Finally, I took my focus off of him and put it on God. Then an awesome thing happened. I learned first hand the power of the Scriptures that if Jesus be lifted up, He would draw all unto Himself. My husband was drawn back into the marriage by the God in me. By the time he died, he had given his life to the LORD and become the loving husband I had given up hope for.

BRIDGES tells my story of becoming a wounded nurturer to my children; a woman who had to learn how to forgive supernaturally; one who received spiritual healing and was finally set free while in the midst of my storms.

And now in *Dancing through the Storms*, I take myself out of the storytelling mode to reveal the love lessons God has taught me in a more straight forward way.

I have been a wife; and now I am a mother, an aunt, a grandmother, etc. To this end, I dedicate myself to speaking to and teaching women about their position in Christ and how to have peace with God. As I minister to others, I am continuously amazed at the power and triumph of God as He transforms, renews, rebuilds and reveals Himself in the midst of storms. Once a woman knows who she is, there is no longer a need for her to get caught up in the aforementioned roles - as each one finds their strength, being and will in serving God through serving others.

Advising Others

"A person persuaded against their will is of the same opinion still."

I received much feedback from readers of BRIDGES who wanted to share their own personal stories of similar and, in some cases, worse abuse. From these stories, I began to realize how important it is to break the silence of abuse within relationships that leave women feeling "used," manipulated and shamed. However, I quickly learned that a woman must be willing to listen and then take appropriate action to break free of abuse.

I want to make it clear that you will not be able to reach everyone you attempt to talk to. Timing is critical. Some have to go through, like the Prodigal Son, and come to the end of self-effort, before being willing to surrender and accept help.

Sometimes it is hard to get someone to listen to you when you try to tell them something that is contrary to what they want to believe. Each is going through a process of grieving the loss of relationship – much like death, and must be ready to accept reality. Most have no frame of reference and feel helpless and indecisive. You must not make their situation worse by seeming callous or giving "in your face" advice.

The worse thing you can do is try to convince someone against their will that they are being abused. They know it by the time you know it. Pride will set in and now they will redouble their efforts to conceal and prove you wrong. You will lose access to them.

You may see someone in a harmful relationship, but know they are not ready to listen to you. No matter how much experience you have had, they believe their situation will be different if they give it enough time. It is better at times like this to just be available and listen.

Victims may have drifted into situations that they wish desperately they had taken more time to think about. Once in such relationships, many times they realize there were warning signs, but either they missed the signs or allowed strong emotions to override the warnings. All too often, wrongly interpreted Scriptures from the Bible keep people in abusive relationship. Another strong motivator to remain is the victim believes they deserve to be abused.

Once deeply involved, the victim does not want to ask for help because of shame or embarrassment, fear of revenge from the perpetrator, or belief that they may be overreacting and can control the situation by changing their behavior. There may be children involved or economic issues that cause them to hesitate and disregard their own safety.

When issues start to occur, they are genuinely puzzled - at a bend in life where they really don't know the questions to ask...or who to ask. Who can I trust? Does he love me or does he not love me? Why is my love not enough? Will things get better or worse? Is it worth hanging in there or should I cut my losses and get out?

Don't take on the responsibility for the total transferring of a victim out of an abusive relationship and through the renewal and rebuilding process. Stay close to God so you won't get drained and burned out. Understand that the long-term health of a victim is in the hands of God, and not you. The God in you is guiding both of you.

It is next to impossible to advise others when it comes to love. Tell them anyway! Just be aware that a person is more likely to respond in anger to your warnings, depending on how deeply they are into a person. Do not take it personally. Tell them anyway. If only one takes your advice, you have done your duty.

This book might be a good starting point to open up dialogue for a resistor. It will be useful for helping a reader identify when behavior is abusive, and when it has become toxic (dangerous to health and welfare). This book can also be used to help its reader recognize through the process of elimination, when it is a relationship they should continue to pursue. Hand them a copy and pray that God will give them that second vision to see what is otherwise hidden from them at the time it is most needed.

Bren Gandy-Wilson

CHAPTER I

The Importance of Being Intentional

Living in a Fish Bowl

"If God is not in charge of your life, then who is?"

Imagine you are on a dance floor waltzing with a partner. The music is a springy tune that makes you think he is Fred Astaire and you are Ginger Rogers. Your partner is smiling down into your eyes as he holds one hand around your waist, and holds your other hand high in the air while he gently twirls you around and around. You giggle in delight. You are young, full of potential and ready to face life head on!

Being in relationship can be compared to being in a dance. Like dancing, it is a give and take process. If he steps forward, you immediately move backwards to keep in step. If he steps to the left or to the right, you must follow. If he moves backwards, you must move forward, and so forth.

However, at what point do you realize that you have given an individual or an organization, or a family member, or even your children the place in your life where only God should be leading? [My sheep hear my voice, and I know them, and they follow me: John 10: 27].

It's at the point where you come to yourself with a gnawing realization that you are not in charge of your life. It's at the point where you feel empty, used and unfulfilled. You are not living life as you feel it is meant to be. It is at the point where you've looked the other way one time too many.

Your thoughts are taking you nowhere. You've become distracted, disillusioned. You feel like you are on a moving train and don't know how to get off – emotional ties, sentimentalities, tradition, obligations and lack of knowledge keep you doing the bidding of others long after the meaning and purpose for doing it is gone.

You keep making excuses and compromising your values long after it is very apparent that the relationship is no longer working for you. In fact, the liaison is not only toxic, but dangerous to your mental, emotional, (and oftentimes physical) well being. Dangerous, as well, to the most important relationship you should have. The greatest commandment is to Love the Lord your God, with all your mind body and soul. And love your neighbor as yourself. Do I love myself? How do I know?

At the point of realizing you are not happy, you may try several techniques for regaining control of your life. First, comes denial; "My life could be much worse." Or "I am committed."

When it becomes apparent that it could be much better, you try to figure out "How did I get to this point? You can make many excuses for your life as it is. "I didn't have anyone to bring me up right; or, my mother (and/or father) was temperamental and unstable?" This being the case, you try going to a doctor who may or may not prescribe tranquilizers to deaden the pain of stress. You may also seek counseling to salve your conscious and make you feel better about not taking responsibility for your own inaction.

Depending on your level of need, you may consider what a significant other has to say about where you are in life and who you have become as a parent, an employee, as a family member, and even as a church member. Their advice, based on what you have revealed, may produce feelings of hopelessness, guilt and even unworthiness for not moving on and letting go. But, what do they know?

So you keep looking for someone who will agree with you that you have a right to feel the way you do. You will talk to anyone and anybody who pauses long enough. You search for someone who understands why you act and feel the way you do. – Someone who can explain that certain theological obligations are not necessary. – Someone who can take away the need to listen to that inner still small voice that urges you to seek God to fill that emptiness. Fear of the unknown keeps you immobile. Like a deer caught in headlights – stuck in indecision, you keep hoping things will change.

In the meantime, you suffer the abuse; you endure the shame and shun that gnawing feeling inside that is urging you to seek your true purpose for being alive. Time is passing you by. "Who would I be without him?" "Where will I go if I leave?" "But what might it be like to follow God's Will for my life - to discover His great plan for creating me?"

But you stay the course. You continue to be involved in unhealthy relationships, waiting for a mythical more opportune time. You tell yourself, "I've already got ten years in this company." How about this one? "He can't live forever, and I don't want to leave my house." Or "I'll make a change when the kids grow up."

Studies show that the mythical time of waiting for kids to mature (not grow up, I said mature), seldom happens in the normal span of 18-20 years. This is especially true of children raised in unhealthy environments. These children are more likely to copy the role model of the abusive parent – the one who never learned to take responsibility for their behavior.

By the time you learn that your indecision to leave is also tied to your indecision to follow God's purpose for your life, there may be innumerable casualties created. Your children have more than likely developed into immature, confrontative, and whiny adults who will continuously lean on their parents for emotional and financial support – unless they find a partner who will put up with them. Then the cycle of abuse begins again. They never seem to get it all together.

As time goes on, your willpower to take control of your own life lessens as you age. Did you know that you can become accustomed to abuse? I think they call it settling or making your peace with the way things are. It is what it is. "I'm too old to make a change." "Who will want me if I leave?" You would rather stay in an abusive and unhealthy relationship rather than risk being alone – or risk having to stand on your own and take care of your own needs.

A story I recently heard may bring these points out more clearly. A pastor went to see a recent widow. As he talked to her about her future, she shared how she had never forgotten her first love. Even after all these years, she thought about him often. She thought about what it would have been like to have been bold enough to get out and seek all God had in store for her rather than to have settled for the meager offerings of unmet emotional needs in the lifestyle she had chosen. Now, her children were strangers and seldom called or visited. She had a gnawing feeling that they had lost respect for her for not standing up for herself – or for them, a long time ago. She felt dissatisfied, discontented.

When asked why she never made the move to get out and go after her dreams, she said "I don't really know. In the beginning everything was alright….until the bills and the drinking started. Then there were other women and his staying away from home. I thought I could change him. I needed to look prettier when he was around. Then the kids came along and I was worried about them. I was tired from working all day. Too tired to worry about what he was doing and with whom. Then I was scared. So I covered the bruises and made excuses. I was too scared to trust my own heart and to go after the life I could have had. It was too tenuous. Better to keep the peace. It would have required a lot more of me than I thought I had to give."

So this widow had never experienced real life as it was meant to be lived. She had settled for a dance that took her no further than the fish bowl rather than being brave enough to make decisions that would have expanded her world to live in the freedom of the ocean.

The Changing World

Women are socialized differently from men. For the majority, from the cradle women are taught that they are incomplete without a man in their life. While boys are given guns, bicycles and soldier uniforms as gifts; girls receive baby dolls, kitchen sets and beauty and hair accessories. Little boys are prepared to be tough and go out and conquer the world; while little girls are prepared to be attractive, homemakers, mothers and nurturers in order to save the world. This feeling of incompleteness will lead a woman to be in a hurry to fill this perceived void. If she is in too big of a hurry, or her clock is ticking, she may accept someone not meant for her and believe she will be able to love and nurture strongly enough to overcome any weaknesses he may have. Unfortunately, this type of thinking, without proper knowledge of free will and deception, may lead her down the road to pain and heartbreak

Although the Bible says, "*A wife of noble character who can find?*" (Proverbs 31:10), nowadays a woman must be very careful about whom she allows to "find" her. In the days of the Bible, marriages were arranged by the fathers and mothers of the bride and groom. Families usually lived close by, which insured that the man was more likely to do the right thing by his wife. To this end, it was a safer bet that the marriage would last.

Nowadays, in modern times, the family structure is fragmented. Many women navigate away from home after high school – into colleges and careers. Women no longer have the protective covering of a close knit family. Therefore, a woman must be very careful to use discernment and play an active role in deciding whom she will allow to "find" her and make her their wife. Times are critical as our economic situation grows increasingly tighter.

Many single men are aging and tiring of the excitement they once craved. They are watching life slowly changing; and all they have to look forward to is an uncertain future alone or with friends whose health and interests are declining as rapidly as their own. No wonder many singles are looking around to find someone they can join their life to. While many are coming with worthy motives, some are coming with a need for deliverance from the spirit of addiction, venereal diseases, mental illnesses, un-forgiveness, bitterness, bad health, unethical habits and unspiritual habits. How can a woman tell the difference between a worthy companion and a destructive one? How can she be sure this is the one?

Abuse Defined

"Teach me Your way, O LORD, And lead me in a level path Because of my foes." Psalm 27:12

Abuse is defined as the systematic pattern of behaviors in a relationship that are used to gain and/or maintain power and control over another. When one defines domestic violence in terms of physical abuse only, then the dynamics that keep these relationships together is not fully understood. Domestic or family violence can take different forms:

Physical: Hitting, pushing, biting, punching, choking or throwing things…
Emotional: cursing swearing, attacks on self-esteem, blaming, criticizing your thoughts feelings….
Psychological: Threatening, throwing, smashing, breaking things, punching walls, hiding things, sabotaging your car.
Sexual: any non-consenting sexual act or behavior; unwanted touching, or incest or rape
Neglect – withholding affection, money, food, health care or other needed care.
Spiritual – Misrepresentation of information and misuse of power. Other synonymous terms used interchangeably are spiritual deception, toxic religion, toxic faith, bad church experiences, spiritual terrorism, church abuse, religious abuse, etc.

It is important to note that many examples can be put into more than one category. I find it helpful to say emotional abuse plays on the persons feelings while psychological abuse alters their reality and sexual often does both.

There are several kinds of abuse and each kind can take many different forms. Our society is so tolerant of abusive behavior that we often do not even recognize some behavior as abusive. Abuse can be divided into four categories.

According to the Office of Justice Program, domestic abuse results in more injuries that require medical treatment than rape, auto accidents, and muggings combined.

Many people think that batterers are violent because they have mental illness, low self-esteem, a genetic defect, a drug problem, or because they lose control of their emotions. Even though any one of these may be true, the primary cause of battering is learned behavior.

Abusive partners use violence to gain POWER AND CONTROL. When they want something, they know how to get it--violence. Abuse works because it maintains control over a woman. She lives in fear of further violence and will alter her behavior to accommodate her abuser's moods, whims and needs, in order to protect herself and/or children. The batterer knows how to use other behaviors in addition to violence to keep the woman isolated and subordinate. Backing up these behaviors with violence makes her escape near impossible. An abuser chooses to batter because the choice is there to make and until quite recently, there have been no consequences for these actions.

A diagram was developed by the Duluth Abuse Intervention Project in the form of a Power and Control Wheel. In the diagram, categories of behaviors used to maintain power and control were described as:

> Using coercion and threats
> Using intimidation
> Using Emotional Abuse
> Using isolation
> Minimizing, Denying and Blaming
> Using Children
> Using male privilege, and
> Using economic abuse.

These behaviors are used together as a system by batterers. The Power and Control Wheel is drawn with violence as the rim and other behaviors as spokes. Just like a wheel, they depend upon and reinforce each other.

Each of these tactics helps the batterer to maintain control over the woman. The tactics are backed up and held together by violence and the threat of violence. The woman is forced to comply with the abuser's demands because of the threat of physical harm.

Each action used by the batterer puts another obstacle in place to prevent her escape. Altogether, this system of behaviors builds barriers to a woman's escape far beyond the physical violence alone.

Any family member can be a victim:
>A child
>A partner or spouse
>An older family member

Victims may suffer:
>Serious injuries – even death
>Stress-related physical problems, including headaches, stomachaches and bedwetting
>Mental-health problems, such as depression, feelings of guilt and worthlessness
>Problems at school or work, including discipline problems and trouble getting along with others.

Abusers may experience:
>Legal problems, fines and jail time
>Loss of family and friends
>Problems at work, including loss of job
>More violent relationships, unless they are willing to seek help for their problem.

Witnesses may experience:
>Great stress. Children who witness abuse may in turn abuse their siblings, and later, their own families, for example.

Be aware of the roots of family Violence

Family violence can happen in families of any social and economic background. No matter what the situation, there is no excuse for family violence. Many people who tend to use violence exhibit the following characteristics:

1) Perpetrators saw or suffered abuse as children. Violence is a learned behavior. Many abusers witnessed or suffered abuse earlier in life.

2) Perpetrators abuse alcohol or other drugs. Alcohol or other drugs do not cause abuse. But they are common factors in violent households.

3) Perpetrators have low self-esteem. Abusers often feel insecure and have a poor self-image. This can lead to frustration – and violence.

4) Perpetrators need to feel powerful. Abuse often grows out of a need to be in control. An abusive person may try to control all areas of home life – such as finances, and where family members go and who they see.

5) Perpetrators have wide mood swings. Abusers may be pleasant one moment and violent the next. In some cases, they may have untreated mental-health problems.

6) Perpetrators blame others. Abusers often deny responsibility for their actions. They may blame the victim for abusive behavior by saying, "It's your fault for making me angry."

7) Perpetrators may have unrealistic expectations. For example, an abuser might become upset or violent if a 2-year-old child spills a glass of milk.

Why violence continues

Victims may feel trapped by:
1) **Fear**. It's common for a victim to be afraid to leave because the abuser has threatened more violence.

2) **Lack of money**. A victim may be financially dependent on the abuser.

3) **Low self-esteem and shame**. Victims often feel worthless as a result of abuse. They may feel ashamed of their family problems.

4) **Feelings of isolation**. Language, culture or religious beliefs may make victims feel there is nowhere to turn for help. Older victims may be confined to their homes.

5) **A desire to "make it better."** Many victims believe that if they try harder, the violence will stop. They make think that leaving means they have failed, especially for repeat marriages.

Help is available!

Many services for troubled families are free or available at low cost. Check your local phone book for local listings.

Law enforcement agencies can be called for intervention or protection.

Shelters offer emergency services, such as short-term lodging, protection and counseling.

Family and social service agencies provide counseling, protection, referrals and legal advice.

Legal aid offices can provide legal help for victims who cannot afford a lawyer.

Hotlines can provide immediate help for victims – and abusers. These include:

1) **The National Domestic Violence Hotline** at 1-800-799-SAFE (1-800-799-7233) or 1-800-787-3224 (TTY)
2) The **Childhelp National Child Abuse Hotlines** at 1-800-4-A-CHILD (1-800-422-4453).

CHAPTER II

What God Meant

Beware lest any man spoil you through philosophy and vain deceit, after the tradition of men, after the rudiments of the world, and not after Christ. Colossians 2:8

The answers to all your most basic questions about how life began and humanity's role in it are found in the Book of Genesis. What is the origin of the world? What is special about human beings? What lies at the heart of male and female identities? Are women subordinate to men? How should we interpret God's response to Adam and Eve after the Fall?

These questions and many others are answered decisively in the first chapter of Genesis. Here, we find affirmation that the universe is not an accident but the creation of God, who has revealed Himself as a Person. God not only created the material world but infused it and all living things with structure and order. The Book of Genesis, chapter I immediately defines what is so special about human beings. And Genesis chapters I and 2 strongly affirm the common identity and equality of men and women.

Men and Women are Created in God's Image
(Genesis 1:26-27)

Then God said, "Let Us make man in Our image, according to Our likeness, let them have dominion over the fish of the sea, over the birds of the air, and over the cattle, over all the earth and over every creeping thing that creeps on the earth. So God created man in His own image, in the image of God He created him, male and female He created them."

"Man" is a term for the whole human race (Gen. 1:26). The Hebrew word translated man is **adam**. This familiar word is also the name of the first man, Adam. In most cases we should understand the term **adam** as "mankind," "human beings," or "humankind."

Both male and female are included in man. When the biblical text (interpreted from Hebrew), wishes to make a gender distinction, the word **'ish** is usually used of male human beings; and the word **'issah** is used of female human beings.

Other Hebrew words are used to make a strong sexual distinction. **Zakar** is used to assert maleness eighty-three times in the Old Testament, and **n'qebah** is used twenty-two times to designate the female.

When God said, "Let Us make man," He was not speaking of male human beings, but of both men and women. Male and female are equally, and alike, man.

All human beings are created in God's image (Gen. 1:27). The biblical text takes great pains to maintain the essential equality of the genders. Notice the phrases in Genesis 1:27:

> God created man (**adam**) in His own image
> Male and female
> He created them

Not only does the text use a word that encompasses all human beings (**adam**), but to avoid any possible misunderstanding, it adds "male and female" and uses the plural "them."

God wants us to understand that men and women share the same essential identity. While there are differences between men and women, these are not differences of essence. The essence of humanity, the thing that sets humankind apart from all other living creatures, is that only human beings have been created in God's image and likeness!

The image of God (Genesis 1:26). Genesis 1:26 uses two Hebrew words to communicate the uniqueness of human beings. In the original text, the two terms, **selem** [image] and demut [likeness] are linked. Together, they make a grand theological statement: Human beings bear the image-likeness of God.

Only human beings possess this amazing gift. While theologians have debated implications of the phrase, we can best understand image-likeness in a simply way. God has revealed Himself as a Person, with all the attributes of personhood. He thinks, plans, remembers, appreciates beauty, establishes priorities, distinguishes right from wrong, makes decisions and carries them out, and so forth. When God made human beings in His image, He gifted us with this same wonderful range of capacities. These capacities of His, reflected in human nature, make us persons too, and constitute the image-likeness of God.

What Genesis 1:27, 28 teach us is that all human beings, men and women, share these gifts equally. Some of us will be more intelligent than others, some more sensitive to beauty. The existence of these and other human capacities, not the amount of any one capacity a person may possess, makes each of us human and reflects something of the glory of a God who possesses every quality to perfection.

What we should always remember as we look into Scripture's teaching on women is that women, equally with men, have been gifted by God with His own image-likeness. The women we meet in Scripture display these gifts just as clearly as do the male heroes of our faith. In essence, men and women are the same.

The Creation of Eve
(Genesis 2:18-23)

One of the truly fascinating passages of Scripture is the report in Genesis 2 of Eve's creation. God created the first man Adam, and placed him in Eden. There, Adam explored the wonders of God's creation. But wherever Adam looked, he was reminded that something was missing. He could not find another creature like himself.

And the LORD God said, *"It is not good that man should be alone, I will make him a helper comparable to him."*

Out of the ground, the LORD God formed every beast of the field and every bird of the air, and brought them to Adam to see what he would call them. And whatever Adam called each living creature that was its name. So Adam gave names to all cattle, to the birds of the air, and to every beast of the field. But for Adam, there was not found a helper comparable to him. And the LORD God caused a deep sleep to fall on Adam, and he slept; and He took one of his ribs, and closed up the flesh in its place. Then the rib that the LORD God had taken from man He made into a woman, and He brought her to the man.

"**A helper comparable**" (Genesis 2:18). One of the fictions upon which the view of women held by some Christians rests is that women were created subordinate beings. The NIV translates this phrase as a "helper suitable for him," offering further support to those who argue that as "helpers," women were created to be subservient to men and to meet men's needs. The implication is that it is men who count and women's concerns are to be subordinate to men's.

But the Hebrew phrase here is *'ezer l'neg'du*, which is best understood as a "helper corresponding to him." Commenting on the phrase, the Expository Dictionary of Bible Words (1985) notes:

> *In Eve, God provided a "suitable helper" (Genesis 2:20). Eve was suitable because she shared with Adam the image and likeness of God – the image that permits human beings to relate on every dimension of personality (emotional, intellectual, spiritual, physical, etc.). Only another being who, like Adam, was shaped in the image of God would be suitable.*

The word for "helper" here is *'ezer*. It means "a help," "a support," "an assistant." Before we understand this concept to imply inferiority or subordination, we should note that the root is used in the Old Testament to speak of God as helper of His nation and of individuals. God is man's helper in all kinds of distresses (Exodus 18:4; Deuteronomy 33:7, 26, 29; Psalms 20:2; 33:20; 70:5; 89:19; 115:9-11; 121:1; 124:8; 146:5; Hosea 13:9). We do not conclude from this that God is inferior to the person He helps.

"**That was its name**" (Genesis 2:19). A fascinating feature in the story of woman's creation is the way God prepared Adam for his mate. The text tells us that God brought Adam every beast and bird to name. In the Old Testament, names were more than labels. Names were understood to capture and express something of the essence of the things named. The implication is that Adam carefully observed each creature over a significant period of time so he might understand something of its peculiar nature. Then Adam assigned that creature a name that accurately reflected that nature.

In the process of carefully studying birds and animals, Adam made a significant discovery. As wonderful as all living creatures were, none among them corresponded to him. There was no creature suited by its nature for him to relate to it.

It was only after Adam had made this discovery, and had begun to feel the emptiness of his isolated life, that God caused him to fall into a deep sleep and set about preparing Eve.

"Flesh of my Flesh" (Genesis 2:23). Genesis 2:23 records Adam's words when God brought Eve to him. We can sense his wonder and excitement. "This at last, is flesh of my flesh!" Since Adam had been assigned by God to name, His name given to Eve would be honored by God.

What Adam is saying, of course, is "Now, at last, here is one who shares my identity – one to whom I can relate because she is everything I am, and I am everything she is. Here, at last, is another person!

Again, we have the strongest kind of biblical affirmation of their essential identity, men and women alike bear the image-likeness of God, and because of it, men and women can relate to each other on every level of the human personality – and also to God.

The creation story in all details strongly affirms woman as the full equal of man. Woman's "otherness" or her inferiority and subordination to man simply is not supported by the story of creation.

Effects of the Fall

While "otherness" and female inferiority cannot be found in the story of creation, some claim to see it in the Scriptural account of the Fall. The theory is that while men and women were created equal, when Adam and Eve sinned, God assigned womankind an inferior place as punishment for Eve's behavior.

So we need to examine closely the consequences of the choice of Adam and Eve to eat the forbidden fruit.

Consequences of the Fall

The two fled silently, desperately. They averted their gaze from each other until they had covered themselves with broad leaves torn from low-lying plants. Then they crept into the bushes to hide.

But they could not hide from Him. They heard His voice calling them, and they cowered deeper into the concealing branches. Once they had loved that voice; now it terrified them. What would He do to them? Truly, as the serpent had promised, their eyes had been opened to good and evil – and they had discovered that now they were evil!

The voice drew nearer. "Where are you?" The branches they crouched behind parted, and the first pair felt His eyes on them. Still crouching, Adam answered. "I heard Your voice in the garden, and I was afraid because I was naked; and I hid myself."

With infinite sadness, the LORD questioned them, heard their excuses, and explained the consequences of their choice to eat the forbidden fruit. God addressed the three central parties separately. To the serpent and the fallen angel who had spoken through him, God said:

> *"Because you have done this, you are cursed more than all cattle, and more than ever beast of the field. On your belly you shall go, and you shall eat dust all the days of your life. And I will put enmity between you and the woman, and between your seed and her seed. He shall bruise your head, and you shall bruise His heel."*

To the woman He said:

> *"I will greatly multiply your sorrow and your conception. In pain you shall bring forth children, your desire shall be for your husband, and he shall rule over you."*

Then to Adam He said,

> "Because you have heeded the voice of your wife, and have eaten from the tree
> of which I commanded you, saying, "You shall not eat of it," Cursed is the
> ground for your sake. In toil you shall eat of it all the days of your life. Both
> thorns and thistles it shall bring forth for you, and you shall eat the herb of the
> field. In the sweat of your face you shall eat bread till you return to the ground.
> For out of it you were taken; For dust you are, and to dust you shall return."
>
> -Gen. 3:14-19

When we look closely at these pronouncements, we note a striking parallelism. Each explanation of the consequences of the Fall has physical, psychological, societal, and spiritual aspects for each of the parties involved.

God curses Satan (Genesis 3:14, 15). Only God's words to the serpent that hosted Satan are identified as a curse. Selah!!! In biblical language, a curse *('atar)* is a binding act and a punishment. In this case, the physical consequences of the curse were visited on the serpent. It must forever crawl on the earth's surface on its belly.

Psychological and societal consequences were visited on Satan, and are expressed in 3:15a. God speaks to the devil of "enmity between you and the woman, and between your offspring and hers." The psychological consequences for Satan as explained here is a settled animosity toward the human race, rooted deep in his essential being. The second phrase, "and between your offspring and hers," directs our attention to a unique relationship between fallen human beings ["your offspring"] and God's Son [her Seed].

The Hebrew word for "offspring" is a collective noun, always found in the singular and never in the plural. Thus we are to understand Satan's "offspring" as humanity itself, alienated from God by the Fall and attuned by the Fall to Satan's voice and his ways. The "offspring" imagery is used throughout Scripture, and is clearly seen in New Testament passages describing unredeemed (un-regenerated) human beings as related to Satan morally and spiritually (compare John 8:44-47; Ephesians 2:2; Colossians 1:21; 1 John 3:10). And evidence of this antagonism is seen in history, for humankind has displayed a marked antipathy to the God of revelation, and a strange attraction to gods of its own invention.

It is important to realize that this enmity has an impact on society. Every culture significantly institutionalizes values and behaviors. These values and behaviors are not only actively hostile to all that which is godly and good, but they are also harmful to human beings. The enmity between God and a world that adopts Satan's values is real indeed, and it is important to discern which values and behaviors reflect Satan's standards rather than God's.

The spiritual consequences to Satan are defined in the last phrases of this verse, "He will crush your head, and you will strike his heel." It is clear from the use of "he' and "his" that "offspring" refer to an individual. What is normally a collective noun is used in a singular sense. One day a Deliverer will come. He will crush Satan and strip him of his power, despite being terribly bruised in the process. Satan will suffer defeat, as through Eve's promised offspring. God acts to set all things right.

God explains the consequences of the Fall for women (Genesis 3:16). When we look at God's words to Eve, we note first of all that she is **not** cursed. Rather, God spells out for Eve the implications of her choice, for herself, and also for all her daughters.

> *"I will greatly multiply your sorrow and your conception. In pain you shall bring forth children; your desire shall be for your husband, and he shall rule over you." – Gen. 3:16*

This verse has long puzzled commentators. The rabbis tended to interpret Genesis 3:16 in a sexual way. Childbirth will be painful. A woman's desires (Heb. *T'shuga*: cravings, hungers, focused intent) have generally been understood as a reference to the conjugal act (as by Rashi and see Midrash; v. Niddah 31b). However, N'Tziv comes closer to the text's meaning when he observes that "in the most literal sense, the woman always strives to find favor in her husband's eyes."

When we look at this verse (Genesis 3:16) carefully, we see that the consequences spelled out to Eve and Satan are parallel. The Fall had a physical, psychological, societal and spiritual impact on Eve. These consequences extended beyond Eve and apply to all her daughters, for in Genesis, Eve represents not just herself but all womankind.

Physical Consequences of Eve's fall. Psychologically, the desires of Eve's daughters now focus on men. The translation "your desire will be for your husband" is unfortunate but understandable. The Hebrew term translated "husband" is *'ish*, which simply means "man." As Adam stands in this passage not only for himself but also for male humanity, the text is better understood as "your urge will be directed toward men." This is not necessarily a reference to sexual desires, but rather a description of the psychological reorientation of women toward seeking to please not just husbands, but men in general. The psychological orientation of Eve's daughters shifted with the Fall so that their urge or cravings, as *teshuga* is best understood, are to please men.

The social consequences of Eve's fall. Societally, this reorientation is expressed in the ways human cultures define men's dominion over women in social institutions, in the family, and even in the Christian church.

The spiritual consequences of Eve's fall. Spiritual consequences of the Fall for women are clearly implied in God's words to Eve. Women, in shifting their urges from a desire to please God to a desire to please males, lose sight of who they have been created to be. The potential for abuse is great with the loss of it identity. Similarly, in exercising a distorted dominion over women, men not only usurp the role of God, but also hold women down and defraud society of the gifts that individual women might bring to enrich all. Men are able to be successful in this area when women don't recognize they have gifts and abilities just as men have.

God explains the consequences of the Fall for men (Genesis 3:17-19). The passage continues with an explanation to Adam of the consequences of the Fall for the human male.

> *Cursed is the ground for your sake. In toil you shall eat of it all the days of your life. Both thorns and thistles it shall bring forth for you, and you shall eat the herb of the field. In the sweat of your face you shall eat bread till you return to the ground. For out of it you were taken. For dust you are, and to dust you shall return.*
>
> – Genesis 3:17b-19

Here again, Adam is not cursed. Rather God explains the consequences of Adam's disobedience.

Physical consequences of Adam's fall. The first physical consequences are death, reflected in mankind's return to dust. Death, as a process of decay and degradation, is also reflected in nature. The beauty we see in nature reflects the goodness of God's original creation. But the pain, struggle, and decay we see corrupting all of God's creation are a consequence of Adam's sin.

Psychological consequences of Adam's fall. Why the repeated emphasis on labor and toil? Because, just as the Fall stripped Eve of her longing for God and replaced this healthy desire with an urge to please men, so Adam was stripped of his longing for God. What has replaced this healthy desire for God in males has been a desire to achieve by their own efforts. The psychological consequences of the Fall in men has been the emergence of a competitive desire to surpass other men – to bend every effort to excel.

Genesis 3 depicts this struggle in agricultural terms and also describes its futility. A man will strive to build; whether kingdoms or companies or fortunes or power, dust awaits the individual. "Dust you are," the text reminds us, "and to dust you will return," leaving every meaningless accomplishment behind.

Societal consequences of Adam's fall. Societally, the urge to excel is expressed as a drive to dominate and control others. Women, whose desire is toward men, are terribly vulnerable to male domination. How ironic it is! Eve used her influence to lead Adam to disobey. As a consequence, the tide of influence has been reversed, and Eve's daughters are carried away on the flood of desires - that urge which makes them desire men's approval.

Spiritual consequences of Adam's fall. Spiritually, men have been corrupted just as women have by the relational reversals of the Fall. Men's desires, which were refocused from pleasing God toward personal achievement and the urge to dominate, have also trapped them psychologically and societally. The satisfaction of the flesh is most important. Rather than having a clear image of what they were created to be, men have replaced God's best with pitiful human substitutes. Even as women have lost their intended identity, men have lost theirs also.

And so, in warping and distorting humanity, the Fall has had a disastrous impact on individual women and men and on the institutions and values of society.

God's words to Satan and to the first pair help us understand the underlying nature of the pressures that increasingly corrupt our society and cause terrible damage to girls and women, as well as distort relationships between them and men. Once we understand these pressures, much that we find in Scripture takes on fresh and new meaning. We realize that notions we have uncritically accepted about the "proper" roles of men and women, and in some cases have even justified as biblical, are far from God's will for a people who have been redeemed and restored in Christ.

Conclusion: God did not curse Adam and Eve but simply explained the consequences to them of their disobedience. He cursed the snake (the sin behind their actions). Spiritually, men have been corrupted just as women have by the relational reversals of the Fall. Men's desires, which were refocused from pleasing God toward personal achievement and the urge to dominate, have also trapped them psychologically and societally. The satisfaction of the flesh is most important. Rather than having a clear image of what they were created to be, men have replaced God's best with pitiful human substitutes. Even as women have lost their intended identity, men have lost theirs also.

> *"Be careful, however, that the exercise of your rights does not become a stumbling block to the weak."* 1 Corinthians 8:9

The distortion of God's ideal for women and for men that were introduced at the Fall are not to be accepted as the norm by Christians. They are to be rejected, and we are to find our way back to God's original ideal.

We can do this by studying Scripture and discovering in its teachings, and in the women whose lives are portrayed there, a clearer vision of what all of us – men and women alike – are to affirm in womankind. Just study how Jesus responded to and lifted women and you will know God's view on the matter. All men and women were created in God's image, and in Christ we are to **recover the equality** and partnership which Adam and Eve lost.

CHAPTER III

A House is not a Home

*"Therefore everyone who hears these words of Mine and acts on them, may be compared
to wise man who built his house on the rock. And the rain fell, and the floods came,
and the winds blew and slammed against that house; and yet it did not fall, for it had been
founded on the rock...." Matthew 7:2-25*

Many spend a lot of care and time in picking out just the right house in the right location and decorating it to suit their personality and lifestyle. But these homes are too weak to bear up under the pressures which will be brought to bear on them without a firm foundation in Christ. We are warned that we must first lay a firm foundation in our hearts and soul. It is necessary to our happiness that we believe in Christ; that we repent of sin, that we live a holy life, that we love one another in order to safely navigate the storms of life. A house is just a building made up of natural materials that keep out weather conditions; but a home is a place for lives to be molded and shaped. It is important for lifetime companions be fortified as believers in Christ and equipped with the Holy Spirit to guide them.

When it comes to a lifetime companion, there are three main types of relationship bonds that may be formed when two people decide to join their lives to each other: Certainly there are hundreds of mutations of these three types, depending on the motives and reactions of the persons involved, but we chose these three broad types to simplify matters and make the point that unless God builds the house, it cannot stand. We call these **three** types Communal, Parasitic and Decadent. These are extreme relationships and quite different from each other for emphasis.

The Communal Relationship

"By Wisdom a house is built, and through understanding it is established; through knowledge its rooms are filled with rare and beautiful treasures." (Proverbs 24:3-4)

Practically speaking, Communal relationship occurs when two human beings interact with mutual motives to the benefit of each other; a Parasitic relationship occurs when two human beings interact, but with the motive of one to live off of and survive through draining the other of its resources; and a Decadent relationship occurs when little intentionality – except satisfying the flesh, is present in either one or both parties – There is harm to both and a fight for survival.

Generally, children born adopt the traditional values and ideas of the family unit they grow up in. They are processed and oriented into the family relationship to reproduce one of the three family unit categories. In the functional Communal family unit, offspring will be taught to interact because they need each other and want to be a part of a loving relationship. They will more than likely adapt the lifestyle Christ commands to enjoy the abundant life as joy and peace reinforce these values.

Figure 1: Communal Relationship represented by both partners having been regenerated.

A communal relationship between individuals exists when both partners benefit. The duty of wives is to stand beside her husband [ideally, this is submission to the Holy Spirit that should reign and rule in the heart of that husband], which includes honoring and obeying him, from a principle of love for him. The duty of husbands is to love their wives.

An example: The love of Christ to the church which is sincere, pure, and constant, notwithstanding her failures is an example of the Communal relationship. Christ gave

Himself for the church that he might sanctify it in this world, and glorify it in the next; that He might bestow on all His members a principle of holiness, and deliver them from the guilt, the pollution, and the dominion of sin, by those influences of the Holy Spirit, of which baptismal water was the outward sign.

The church and believers will not be without spot or wrinkle until they come to glory. But those only who are sanctified now, shall be glorified hereafter. The words of Adam, mentioned by the apostle, are spoken literally of marriage; but they have also a hidden sense in them, relating to the union between Christ and his church. It was a kind of type, as having resemblance. There will be failures and defects on both sides, in the present state of human nature, yet this does not alter the relationship. All the duties of marriage are included in unity and love. And while we adore and rejoice in the condescending love of Christ, let husbands and wives learn hence their duties to each other. Thus the worst evils would be prevented, and many painful effects would be avoided.

A wife gives peace and love to her husband, and in return he shares affection, food and shelter. Thus, everybody wins! A cohesive family team is formed when Christian principles become a functioning part of the relationship. When the authority of Christ is invited in marriage, it brings untold blessings. Therefore, a Godly marriage relationship becomes more than the sum of each individual who makes up the marriage. One plus one equals three! A **synergistic relationship** is formed. The term *synergy* comes from the <u>Greek</u> word *synergia* συνεργία from *synergos*, <u>συνεργός</u>, meaning «working together». This is the positive process of becoming in relationship. Synergy is two or more things functioning together to produce a result not independently obtainable.

Christ in the marriage becomes the ability of the relationship unit itself to outperform even its best individual member as each spouse says "Yes LORD" in unpredictable circumstances. In other words, neither the husband nor the wife believes either is better without the other.

The Parasitic Relationship

"For every house is built by some man; but he that built all things is God." Hebrews 3:4

A Parasitic relationship exists when one party benefits and the other is harmed. This may happen when one partner is committed and the other is not. A Parasitic Relationship is formed when one partner comes into the relationship with less than pure motives. For example, the victimized partner may provide a covering to keep a gay lifestyle hidden. Or they may have money or hold economic security, etc. Deception, infidelity, covert behavior, neglect of meeting the basic needs of their partner, and the use of weapons of humiliation, embarrassment, violence, shameful pointing out of weaknesses in body structure, speech, and lack of education is used for control as one is out to "win" and the other partner is severely damaged. A victimized partner may decide to stay and take abuse because of love, children, economics, fear, lack of a means to support, shame, aged or poor health; and hope positive change or – at the most extreme – death will occur over time to break the cycle. Hence, there is lack of care or false love shown.

Figure 2: Parasitic Relationship represented by only one partner having been regenerated.

If divorce occurs, one partner may fight to get everything and leave the other worse off than when the relationship began. It may be said that one partner has preyed on the other to better their lot in life. One partner becomes a victim and may be left severely broken and bruised. Children in this type of family unit have a 50-50 chance of adapting to either partner's mindset.

Second Timothy three and six paints a vivid picture of the Parasitic Relationship style that may occur when Godly wisdom is absent:

"For among them are those who worm their way into homes and captivate silly and weak-natured and spiritually dwarfed women, loaded down with [the burden of their] sins [and easily] swayed and led away by various evil desires and seductive impulses.,…" (Amplified Bible)

Case Study: Reaping where he has not sown.

A composite profile of the "those" referred to in Second Timothy three and six: "Those" are men who have learned the art of manipulation, illusion and deception with the single goal of "winning the confidence of vulnerable women. Their sole purpose is to make these women take care of them – long term or temporarily, until they move on to their next vulnerable victim. Thus, the nurturing instinct is brought out in women who see a man struggling with lack of transportation, means of earning money, etc.

This type of man is very confident, easily bored and requires high maintenance. They are usually arrogant with bigger than life egos and goals, charismatic, self-absorbed and blame circumstances and everyone else but themselves.

Since women are nurturers, "those" men usually have a unique story of why they are without resources—my mama or my last woman, etc.—that tug at the heart strings. "But I have a feeling I will listen to you," is the general statement that will draw their victim in to believing they are the lucky one who gets to change this one into something better.

For example, by the age of 50, one man (we'll call Phantom), has lived with as many as 25 different women. Each relationship lasted from 3 months to 3 years, depending on the wisdom and ultimate ability of the woman to see through him. Each woman helped him understand better what women like and what women want out of a relationship. He was always and forever in the blush of a new and exciting relationship where he was pampered and smothered with gifts, favor and attention; taken to expensive dinners and on vacations around the world; and forever being introduced to new and oftentimes influential people – all at the woman's expense. All of this is in exchange for his ever increasing ability to listen attentively and respond to a woman's physical, psychological and emotional need to be heard and appreciated.

Phantom never has to worry about paying a bill or having access to a vehicle or all the luxuries available in a comfortable home. He chooses his women well. He studies as much information as they are willing to provide. While the woman works to support the relationship, he will pretend to look for a job. Unaware to his present woman, his looking includes checking dating services in the newspaper and on the internet to initiate contact with his next intended victim.

Because love is in the eye of the beholder, it is hard to give a standard description of this type of man. One woman's trash is another woman's treasure. However, a general description might include one who knows how to dress to impress, a smooth talker, a great lover (not just sexually) – but one who has mastered the art of engaging in great conversation (a listening ear), and gives foot and body massages that would rival the world's finest spas. He has learned to cook romantic meals from when "his woman" comes home exhausted after a hard day's work. He is usually charismatic and prefers women friends to men.

Phantom makes a point of getting along with her children and especially her mother. But as soon as he feels comfortable in the relationship (he feels he has totally won over his victim), he will start to gradually change his repertoire, routine and personality – which is easy since the personality he first introduced as himself was a fake.

Now he starts to relax and enjoy himself as the real him. At first changes are subtle. He will test the waters by letting a few curse words slip to see if there is a reaction. He may abuse alcohol and hit the woman and see if she is able to accept, "I'm sorry." As a live-in, he changes the physical environment to accommodate his taste. He changes furniture around and, in the process searches the woman's personal home files (and breaks into computer passwords) to gain access to personal information that he may later take and devour. He becomes stealth, surreptitious in his behavior and veiled about revealing personal information.

Next, he starts to mar the woman's image and new found confidence by complaining about her looks, her speech and her size. He will become uncooperative about spending time in things that he once participated in to pleasure her; and with people and relationships that they use to enjoy. He has her now so he no longer feels a need to do anything he did in the "drawing in" stage.

In an effort to impress her, he starts to brag about other relationships and perhaps illegal activities that he has gotten away with in the past. He is warning her that he is struggling with a spirit of lust – but he is working on it. His motivation for this kind of behavior is to gradually make things so uncomfortable that the woman will eventually be enslaved and confused about what is right and what is wrong. (Isaiah 5:20)

At this point, the woman will typically redouble her efforts to gain back the utopia that is fast slipping away by increasing her spending on herself and on him. The harder she tries, the less cooperative he becomes; intentionally sabotaging the relationship because it is going to be his way or no way. Once she sees her efforts are not working, she is totally bewildered because she doesn't know the game plan. She can't understand why he has flipped and doesn't seem to want "all this" – the love nest and all she has to offer him.

She will try different strategies from reasoning with him to allowing herself to be provoked into attacking him back, making it easy for this bad boy to justify stealing her blind and pawning whatever he can get for maintaining the "pay as you go" card that she does not know exists. He came looking and will leave looking if necessary. Nothing will get in the way of his getting all he can get from this relationship before he moves on to the next conquest that he has spent weeks and perhaps months grooming for his arrival.

This type of man has been called many names. In Proverbs he is called a fool; in modern times, he is called everything from playboy, no-good, gigolo, bad boy, parasite to professional con man and/or demonic.

The most sobering fact is that Phantom is not alone; there are millions of bad boys who have mastered the skill of beguiling women to get their needs met. Some bad boys are single, while many others are married. But that fact has never stopped them from looking and taking up new challenges. "Worming their way" into the hearts of weak women may be said to be as challenging and fulfilling a sport as any other.

A composite profile of the type of "**silly and weak natured and spiritually dwarfed women**" Paul refers to in second Timothy three and six that a bad boy picks is usually one of low self-esteem (known to her or unknown). She believes she has overcome or is overcoming whatever childhood traumas or relationship abuses she has encountered through the grace of God. She may be a titled person in the church or a professional businesswoman. She is one who receives great satisfaction through personal achievement.

Many of these women have sought refuge in the church; some in power careers. Out of gratitude to God, she is ready to help "save" the world. She believes she is now equipped to handle anything. She may be isolated from close family because of past hurts. In an effort at humility, most, but not all, see themselves as not very pretty, heavy set, etc. On the other hand, many women have spent years grooming themselves to attract men. Whatever the situation, she feels a particular sense of pride in such a handsome and obviously intelligent man, such as this bad boy, showing an interest in her! She immediately starts to make plans to incorporate him into her life (and perhaps ministry); many without prayer or sincere prayer and waiting on God for an answer. After all, isn't it obvious that this is the one?

In the beginning of the relationship, the woman's interest in her appearance skyrockets. She starts to exercise and diet in an effort to watch her weight. As the relationship progresses, inhibitions are lowered and she starts to dress more provocatively. People who knew her before start to comment on how good she looks; she is "simply glowing." Interests in outside activities and girlfriends that use to bring her a great deal of personal satisfaction, begin to drop off. Everything now begins to center around this man—and keeping him happy. She feels blessed to be in relationship – part of a couple. God surely has smiled on her!

In the honeymoon period, she experiences the ideal companion. This bad boy is willing to do whatever it takes to make her happy and pull her deeper into him. He listens to her and makes all her fantasies come true – within limits. This type of man relies heavily on verbal feedback from the woman about her family, job, children, etc. in order to gain control over her emotions and manipulate her behavior. He loves whatever she loves! Her favorite foods are his favorite foods. If she has advertised for a man of God, then he comes as a man of God. If a businessman, then he comes as a businessman. Whatever she wants, he will become.

At first, she does not notice that he is using her money, her car, her credit cards, etc. His wardrobe is beginning to rival hers. She does not notice that he is taking his time about finding a job and beginning to spend more and more quality time on the computer, cell phone or away from home.

He will gradually manipulate and isolate her from anybody who threatens to expose what he is really doing. He will lie about close girlfriends making passes at him, accuse her children of stealing from her and even make passes at her mother, aunts, etc.; and may actually begin a close relationship with one of these women – spreading confusion, fear and distrust, all in an effort to divide and conquer.

If people begin to see through him, it will be their word against his. By now, the woman is more willing to give up her career, friends and family and lower her standards in an effort to prove to him that she really loves him. She is willing to make compromises. As one woman put it, "I don't care if he doesn't work. As long as he is here when I get home and willing to fix things around the house and cook, he can stay with me." How sad because she doesn't know his true agenda. She just gave this bad boy additional rope to take his time in hanging her.

Many women attempt to reform and understand the background of these bad boys, forgetting that if God has not been able to change them, she has little chance. It would never occur to her that bad boy doesn't want to change. Change what? He likes who he is and what he is doing! Without spiritual discernment (1 Cor. 2:14), he hasn't a clue as to what she is talking about?

Once she catches on to "something is wrong," she just can't believe he is actually doing these things to her! "Look at all I've done for him; how good I've been to him." "Perhaps he doesn't know any better." "Perhaps, he didn't know real love growing up." She forgets that certainly others have prayed; others have cried and pleaded; others have forgiven and attempted understanding—all to no avail. Why, because God will not touch his free will.

If their agenda is not met, some bad boys will actually go through with marriage, knowing full well they do not truly love their bride or intend to stay with them "till death do us part." When this happens, the woman has something bad boy has not gotten yet.

Speaking of marriage, Phantom has been married five times. He has never bothered to get a divorce, but just up and leaves. Many bad boys escape in the woman's vehicle, and can be gone for days before she realizes he has abandoned her because "those" men don't mind leaving their clothes and most everything she bought him. She keeps looking at all of his things still in place and believing he will return. In the case of marriage, once they decide on, or is forced into "divorce," those men will attempt to take half of what has been gathered through legal means.

When bad boy finally leaves, the woman may have lost her reputation, her money, her good credit and close relationships with family and friends. In an even worse scenario, she may lose her job, her house, etc., and she may have a hard time rebounding and need to seek professional counseling for emotional support.

Now here's the thing, many grieve the loss of the bad boy after he is gone. Without counseling some women may intentionally weigh out "better with him than without him." Many will lose sleep; go on medication for depression and replay the good parts of their relationship with bad boy - calling evil good and good evil - all in an effort to convince themselves that things really were not as bad as they seemed.

Bad boys may enter, leave and reenter some women's lives until something happens to make it impossible for them to return. The woman may finally get married or move to where she can't be found. Wonder of wonders, some bad boys do become saved, but it is very, very rare. Most will go until they end up in jail, sick or dead. Either way, you shouldn't miss the fact that the judgment of God is ever present. He is too wise to make a mistake and too loving to be unfair.

The Decadent Relationship

"The wise in heart accept commands, but a chattering fool comes to ruin." Proverbs 10:8

A Decadent relationship exists when both parties are harmed. The family unit is totally fragmented, a constant battleground. The home environment may be compared to the survival of the strongest. This symbiotic relationship is mostly demonstrated when one or both partners do not honor or believe in the marriage vows. Usually, but not always, partners in a Decadent relationship are physically drawn together, but do not understand what it means to be in covenant relationship.

Figure 3: Decadent Relationship represented by neither partner having been regenerated.

Children brought into this type of family unit are usually harmed physically, emotionally, psychologically, and sexually. Any injury a victimized parent suffers may also be suffered by the child as well. Oftentimes, the victimized parent is abused economically and emotionally. The children are affected by a lack of resources intentionally withheld resulting in lack of food, clothing, proper shelter and other basic needs; limited or no medical attention; poor supervision and, possibly, frequent abandonment.

While all batterers do not sexually abuse their children, many do. If the child is sexually abused by the parent, it is called incest. Some adults shift the blame to the child. Adults are always, always responsible for the abuse. Adults have power over children, not the other way around. The physical results of sexual abuse can include injury to the genital area or other body parts, venereal disease and/or pregnancy.

Whether the child is a direct target of emotional abuse (e.g., yelling, name-calling), or witnesses domestic violence in any form, between family members, the effects are devastating and long lasting. even into the affected child's own adult relationships, without counseling. Without divine intervention, children will adapt the Decadent relationship style of living.

The Decadent relationship allows the cares of the world to come in, control and ultimately destroy peace and harmony. Victimized partners and children usually react with intense feelings of sadness, anger, fear, confusion, self-blame and insecurity. They isolate and become withdrawn. Behavior may vacillate from being aggressively defiant to passively compliant; there is a limited tolerance for frustration; low self-esteem, poor social skills, and poor problem-solving skills. These things manifest in bills always being behind, creditors calling; Lights, water and telephone regularly disconnected with high reconnection fees.

Children may take on adult roles and behaviors; exhibit violent behavior toward other children, pets, and toys; and there is a greater risk for drug abuse, sexual acting out, delinquent behavior, and running away.

<u>Case Study:</u> I can do whatever I want to do!
(Except taken from *Women are Spiritual BRIDGES, pp. 88-91*)

Nambi was very young, beautiful, and innocent about the ways of the opposite sex. One night she met Ceejay, a very confident and arrogant young man, in a bar. After one conversation, Ceejay knew she was naïve and set his sights on her. After meeting him, her mother tried to warn Nambi that this man was nothing but trouble. When she asked her mother why she felt that way, her mother just said "I've been living a long time and I sense that this young man is no good for you."

Nambi didn't like her mother's explanation. She was sure her mother just didn't want her to be happy. She felt her mother was envious of her good fortune at having found someone whom she loved and who loved her back – and was good looking to boot! She warned her mother to either accept Ceejay or she would cut her out of her life!

After a few months, Nambi moved out of her mother's house and in with Ceejay. At first, things went very well. Nambi cooked, cleaned and went to work. She was very happy! But, after a while, Nambi learned that Ceejay was selling drugs. He also had a violent temper. He would slap Nambi around for the slightest disagreement – the food wasn't cooked right, or the house wasn't cleaned the way he liked it.

Nambi didn't like the fact that Ceejay didn't work and there was always other people hanging around their place. She began to regret that she had not listened to her mother. She wished more and more that she was back in the peace and privacy of home, but she was too ashamed to admit to her mom, or anyone else, that she had been wrong about Ceejay. She begins to wish she had never met him.

Nambi became increasingly afraid of Ceejay's moods and bad temper until finally, she made up her mind that she wasn't going to take it anymore. She secretly made plans to pack her things and leave town. In the meantime, she discovered CeeJay's hiding place for his drug money. One night, she crept out while CeeJay was out with the boys. She breathed a sigh of relief when she boarded a bus out of town.

When CeeJay discovered that both Nambi and his money were missing, he became livid with rage! He assumed she had gone back home to live with her mother. He walked the floor and stewed and stewed until that night when the house was dark; he crept through the window of Nambi's mother's house and waited for them to come home. Nambi's mother had gone to Bible Study that night. She still didn't know that her daughter had left town.

Perhaps because it was dark, CeeJay couldn't tell that it was Nambi's mother and not Nambi who came through the door. Nambi and her mother were about the same height and build. CeeJay attacked the mother with a knife, stabbing her over and over in the chest and slashing her face and neck. He left her lying in a pool of blood on the living room floor. He then set the house on fire.

The police were able to put two and two together and CeeJay was eventually caught and sentenced to life in prison. Last heard, Nambi had attempted suicide twice and was living in a mental institution. Her brothers and sisters were still very angry with her. They felt that their mother would still be alive if Nambi had thought about others and listened to her mother's advice about CeeJay in the first place. Now, ask yourself the following questions:

1. Was being young a good reason for Nambi to ignore her mother's advice?
2. When it became obvious she had made a mistake, what caused Nambi not to seek her mother's help?
3. What caused Nambi's mom to "sense" that this young man was no good?
4. Had you been Nambi's mom, how would you have handled Nambi?

Conclusion: All human existence is connected to these three basic types of relationships sooner or later. In order to guarantee continued existence, humans take full advantage of the resources that God has provided. Without Christ to regulate lifestyles, these resources and the people who adapt to them, may be perverted and misused.

Both Parasitic and Decadent relationships exist to allow partners to take advantage of one another and to use each the other for certain purposes. Both relationships may last only for reasons of children, shared wealth, business partnerships, etc., but parasitic relationships are easily broken and entered into again and again. Both relationships have the potential to breed physical violence, disrespect, dishonesty and emotional/psychological abuse.

While human beings have a need to mate and procreate for survival, the fall of man caused this need to become perverted. Human symbiosis is a process, and with inbreeding, a cyclical one.

CHAPTER IV

Journey towards Becoming Connected

"Shall I bring to the point of birth and not give delivery?" says the LORD.
Or shall I who gives delivery shut the womb?" says your God." Isaiah 66:9

As human beings, we are part of the whole of humanity. Born into a world limited by time and space; we experience our own thoughts, feelings and emotions as something separate and apart from the rest of humanity. It feels like an optical illusion of our own consciousness. This illusion is a kind of prison for us, restricting us to our own personal desires and affections. The self is a complex set of interactions experienced through the five senses. The human baby is consumed with discovering its hands, fingers, toes, etc. We experience taste through eating and connect with the physical world around us; crawling, holding toys, pulling up, falling, and getting back up; listening to and reacting to caregivers, etc. In the beginning, it is easier to relate to things than to people.

As we grow and experience the dynamics of others (call it community), we try to come to terms with a growing sense of awareness that we are totally alone in a kind of darkness, even in the midst of others. We start to yearn for connection - to make sense of this growing need. When there is vast information flowing in and out of our consciousness, we are being drawn towards becoming a part of this whole. How can we feel alone when there are others all around us? We give this "whole" a name, we call it the Universe.

"….that the hour has come for you to wake from sleep." Romans 13:11

If we are blessed, we will somehow begin to connect this Universe with becoming aware of a God who loves us; a God who, while all powerful, all knowing and omnipresent, is desperately calling out to us – drawing us ever nearer to recognizing His presence; His love for us. We will begin to look within to a God whose task He has made it to deliver us from our prison of darkness. We may, in the beginning experience this awareness, this drawing, as a knowing – which may be interpreted as a part of our selfish optical illusion. We analyze, evaluate, role play, seek balance and set goals as the mind begins to interact more and more with the world and the people who enter and exit our world. Still, there is persistent love, a persistent Presence, unlike any other we can ever experience in any other way. There is also a growing need for clarity and to adopt belief systems as we struggle to experience life in all its complexity.

Our task then, becomes freeing ourselves from this self-made optical prison through a heightened awareness of a God who is bent on calling attention to His existence; and by widening this connection of love, of compassion - this Love that we sense is intelligent and purposeful, but we do not completely understand where all this knowing is coming from. What is it I know? How do I know what I know?

In our wondering and seeking, we have begun our journey of discovery that we are not alone. God exists. He is a God who is beginning a good work in you. What is THE STORY and what is my part in it? Why am I here? What is my eternal destiny? What am I suppose to do with this knowledge? How am I to fit my belief systems and the people who taught them to me into my new experiences? God wants to take us from the law to faith. He does this thru allowing suffering in our life. If we respond in faith, there are untold blessings.

If we are obedient to the drawing, we start to" get it." We come to know beyond a shadow of a doubt that we are not alone. And our life can never be the same. We will discover that we are created in the image of God with a God-shaped hole that only He can fit in. Now we are on a journey to discovering God's purpose for our life. Our task then changes, as we abide in His Word, to reaching out to others and embracing all living creatures and the whole of nature in its beauty and majesty with the same love we have been freely given. We become portable churches.

We will continue this reaching out (as a baby reaches forth for its mother, its first human contact). We will not be able to achieve the plans God has for us apart from connecting with others. Community is necessary to finding significance and reaching our goals. The effort for such achievement starts to free us to become a part of the liberated whole, which will become our foundation for an inner sense of transformation and security.

This reaching out will lead us into our own distinct personality as we experience the world and the people with whom we interact. As we age, the reaching out becomes less general and more specifically directed towards finding that special person to continue the journey that we began at birth.

Attaching to Others

"A man that has friends must show himself friendly: and there is a friend that sticks closer than a brother." Proverbs 18:24

Many examples of attachments are found in God's creation. Plants are attached to soil. Fish are attached to or contained in water. Human beings are attached to this planet because of a need for an oxygen-rich environment. There is also a need to be attached to other humans. Remember the first man Adam could not find another creature in all creation like himself; so God said "It is not good for the man to be alone." [Genesis 2] Thus God was declaring man's need for human attachment.

What do you want from me? What do I want from you? What are the implications for how we treat each other once we are saved? If we read the Bible from cover to cover we easily come to the conclusion that the Bible is a book that talks about two major relationships-- God and man and man and man. One of the major aspects of being alive is that we are able to enter into relationships that are fun, exciting, and warm. These relationships are called **Phileo** or friendships. Christians are to become "good" friends with God and good friends with each other.

Who are you? Who am I? In the initial phase of a relationship these questions are answered. Who I am is largely what I think and how I respond to you, others and my environment. The same is true for you. Getting to know you and others is what life is all about. In order for me to know you, you must "open up" to me and feel comfortable in doing so. I must do the same. Unfortunately, if you do not understand and appreciate yourself (that does not mean you narcissistically love yourself), you will not accept and appreciate me. There are two extremes to avoid in relationships, "wonderfulizing" ourselves or others and "demonizing" ourselves or others. This means we need balance.

Balance is important. Relationships grow rapidly during their initial stages, probably because there is a certain excitement called "discovery" about creating new friendships. And then, most of us value highly friendships that we can open up in. However, opening up does not mean we have to go into "gory" details about our past. It means letting others know what we think about current situations.

The more open and self-disclosing we are in our conversations with others, the more likely others will like us. This is true because of commonalities that all humans experience. You like broccoli? Well, so do I! Imagine that!

Self-disclosure should be honest, genuine and unaffected by hoping the other person will judge us negatively. If not, we will become estranged from our true selves as we strive to keep up the false impression we have created of our true selves. Self- disclosure should be reciprocated by the person we disclosed ourselves to, or there will be a tendency to feel vulnerable, exposed and not open up any further.

To be sure, there is a certain amount of risk involved in opening up to others. How we respond to the other's self-disclosure can either build or destroy the relationship. This is where Christians need to be very careful. Many of us can be extremely judgmental, damning and condemning. Acceptances, understanding and warmth build a relationship. Try to avoid strong disagreements in new relationships. Damning and condemning expressed in statements like, "How could you do that!" tend to help their recipients think they have committed the unpardonable sin. The recipient of such statements will usually soon leave the relationship in a self-righteous tirade. He or she has become too good to associate with a "dirty low-down sinner."

God reveals (self-discloses) Himself as our Creator Father and best friend. We can trust Him. He knows every aspect of our past and has not rejected us because of it. He looks beyond our faults to meet our needs. We may give up on ourselves, but Scripture promises that God never will give up on us.

Trust is Important. The development and nurturance of trust is important in any relationship because it is foundational. Relationships are not enjoyable if there is a lack of trust. They become uncomfortable. Abraham was a good friend of God. "I know my servant Abraham that he will do all that I ask him." Trust is essentially the knowledge that we will respond to the other person in a positive manner. To build strong friendships people need to know we will accept them. "I know my friend Mike will treat me fairly. He will not reject me if he finds out I have "flaws."

35

For you to like me and me to like you, we must trust each other (do not confuse this kind of trust with what the Bible says about trusting a man for salvation). If we tell the details of another's' self-disclosure, that may be construed as being untrustworthy. The most effective means of communicating trust is through the expression of affection for another. Telling people we like them, smiling, sharing experiences, and hugging create trust. Silence is not "golden" in relationships. It tends to be perceived as indifference at best and rejection at worst. If we do not communicate with people to the extent they communicate with us, they will not trust us.

What should we expect? Each person brings to a friendship certain expectations. These expectations can be simple or complex. Unfortunately, most of us are only vaguely aware of these expectations. Nevertheless, when people meet our expectations, we generally tend to appraise them highly. We like people that do the things that we want them to do. When people stop doing the things we want, we change our appraisal towards the negative. The friendship becomes less enjoyable.

We can think of friendship as a bank account into which friends deposit and withdraw from. If care is not paid to the balance, it can easily go out of kilter. If we make the mistake of only taking from the account, there won't be anything for the other person. The account becomes unbalanced. The relationship is then in trouble. Put simply, friendships deteriorate because people don't get what they want from them. If we want to make a relationship last, we had better determine what our friend wants from the friendship and try to give what he wants. For the friendship to be balanced, both partners must get a significant amount of what they want from the relationship. Therefore, it's important that both partners keep a watchful eye on the "balance."

Suppose a friend treats you to lunch several times. He is depositing into the friendship account. Naturally, you feel warm and good because it's nice to be treated to lunch. Perhaps you would not go to lunch because you could not afford it if you were not treated. Your friend pays because he may want your company. A heart-felt thanks would be in order. But, if your friend perceives that you have the money but are simply too "tight" to reciprocate, your friendship account will soon be out of balance. Continue to take without giving and you will find your friend negatively responding to you and eventually avoiding you.

Just as a farmer does not plant seeds without expecting to get something in return, so, people do not give and give without expecting something in return. We keep a mental record of our transactions with others. Too many withdrawals from the friendship account without deposits and the friendship will be in trouble. That's reality!

Basic Wants. There are some basic things that people want from friendships -- honesty and integrity go without saying. There is nothing that will unbalance a friendship quicker than lies and dishonesty. Keep your word if you possibly can. If you have to break a promise, let your friend know why. Most people understand enough to know that we can't always do what we say.

Another requirement for good friendships is time spent together. Spreading yourself too thin makes you everybody's friend and nobody's friend.

Anger has no place in friendships. We can say some nasty things when we are heated. Anger is one of the best ways to wipe out a friendship account. If you have a problem with anger, work on it. But, leave it out of your friendships. It is more effective to calmly disagree and discuss a subject than to display anger. Replace anger with "appropriate concern."

Understanding and Acceptance. More than any other characteristic in a relationship, people want to be understood and accepted. When a friend has a struggle with something that matters a great deal to him but he hasn't overcome, behaving non-judgmentally will create more appreciation in our friend than we might imagine.

People often play a game in their mind called "If they knew." They muse, "If they knew 'this' about me, they probably wouldn't be my friend." The person is attempting to determine if the friendship can withstand reality (that people are fallible, flawed creatures). Many friendships end because God has not made people as "perfect" as we think they ought to be. That's something we really need to think about. Encouraging a person to overcome a weakness is fine. Insisting, by our attitude that someone must overcome a weakness - or turn it into a lifelong obsession - puts a lot of stress on a relationship. Disappointment soon follows, when our "great expectations" are not met!

Enjoyable Friendships. What makes a truly enjoyable and long lasting friendship? The answer is affection. Friendships thrive on it. Telling people we like them, giving them a "bear" hug or doing some other nice act goes a long way to make friendship blossom. We like people that are thoughtful, considerate, kind hearted, understanding--nice. If you would build a friendship, be nice. A card, a gift, a letter, praise, and appreciation keep the friendship account full.

If he thinks an anniversary is the most important time of the year to him, we had better play up that day as much as we can. Get him a gift, cook him all of his favorite things for dinner and attempt to satisfy his every whim. If he likes roast and potatoes on his birthday, we had better do our best to make sure he gets just that. It may be a challenge to figure out what our friend's desires are, because we are all different. However, figuring out what another person's desires are and then trying to reasonably satisfy them goes a long way in keeping a friendship balanced and happy and can be great fun because we share in their joy.

<u>The BEST types of friends</u> are those that can stand on their own two feet (male or female), and make an effort to be mentally healthy. The psychologically healthy individual is able to be happy with or without things (as was the Apostle Paul). He or she desires and usually has several good friends or can have a main friend as a marriage partner. They have the green-eyed monster under control. He or she is jealous in the sense they want to continue an enjoyable partnership, but they are not overly jealous. As long as friends spend enough time with each other, they don't mind their friends having other interests--which can mean hobbies or other friends. If he likes Monday night football—she sees no threat in letting him enjoy that while she spends an evening with the girls or does something else that interests her.

<u>What Works?</u> What makes people stay in a relationship is the balance in their friendship account. Our attitude had better be one of willingness to give value for value or we will not succeed in maintaining a friendship. People divorce people that are snotty, un-thoughtful, constantly taking without giving, demanding, un-negotiable, mean spirited, and "right!" If you want to avoid ending a friendship, check your attitude; adjust it if it is out of line. Above all, keep your friendship account balanced.

And the Two Shall Become One

As the Scriptures say, "A man leaves his father and mother and is joined to his wife,
and the two are united into one." Ephesians 5:31

When a unique man and a unique woman come together in Holy Matrimony, something that has never existed before is created; something is wrought that is exciting and challenging and awaits God's Hand on the Potter's wheel. Marriage is made on three planes. The first plane (eros) is the physical plane and is fulfilled in the sexual relationship. The second plane (phileo) is the mental and psychological relationship and relates to companionship/friendship areas of marriage. The third plane (Agape) is the spiritual relationship and is enjoyed when Christians marry Christians. All three aspects must be present for the union to last. A delicate balance must be maintained so that the gifts and talents of each can be fully realized and used for the strengthening of the marriage, the raising of children and the up building of the Kingdom of God.

Playing Roles. Too often married friends think they own each other. They stop being friends and start playing a role called "husband and wife!" The idea that another person is property is as pernicious as the day is long. When people stop getting what they want from a friendship they often start to manipulate the other partner by claiming ownership. It rarely works for long, because we are autonomous. Sometimes, people will even use the laws of God to try and make their partner do what they "demand." Unfortunately, demands don't exactly endear us to others. Realistically, relationships are largely voluntary. That's something we best realize. If we don't have the other person's heart, all the threats in the world are not going to make the relationship work.

A woman should not expect a man to give her life. She should go out and make one for herself. God gave her life and Scripture tells us He is a jealous God. "Thy shalt have no other God before Me". Unfortunately, many Christians have gullibly swallowed the idea that a mate is supposed to "complete" them. This erroneous idea causes many disasters in relationships. With a little reasoning, we can readily expose this lie. The Bible says that a woman was to be a helper for a man. A helper is someone who helps out where the help is desired. The stronger and more independent the helper is, the more desirable her help will be. How you gone help someone else if you are so needy yourself?

When we are "needy," someone that tries to fill our sick "needs" will get tired pretty quick. Half-there people make poor friends and they drain us of our energy and strength. They require constant attention, are usually obsessed with themselves, spend an inordinate amount of time concerned with talking about and having their own sick "needs" met, and therefore have little time to devote to anything--let alone help someone else.

The most enjoyable relationships we can have are ones that start and remain friendships. If we keep our friendship accounts balanced, they will last us our entire life! Learning to be a good friend leads to being a good marriage partner.

Transformation Happens in Relationship. Marriage should be a spiritual as well as an emotional and physical union. The New Testament says that believers should not marry unbelievers (2 Corinthians 6:14). Such marriages cannot have unity in the most important issues in life – commitment and obedience to God. Because Marriage involves two people becoming one, faith may become an issue, and one spouse may have to compromise beliefs for the sake of unity. Many people discount this problem only to regret it later. How will children be taught and will worship be carried out? Don't allow emotion or passion to blind you to the ultimate importance of marrying someone with whom you can be united spiritually. Without the Holy Spirit controlling a life, this person is not under authority to deal with you honestly and faithfully or provide needed financial support. It's "anything goes" or "as long as I am not bored."

"… and they shall be one flesh." Genesis 2:24

Selfishness is an enemy to marriage. Couples are transformed in relationship. The personal self as it was before marriage can no longer exist without threatening unity. Unity occurs through intimacy. Intimacy is the mystical bond of friendship, commitment and understanding that almost defies explanation. It occurs when a man and woman, being separate and distinct individuals, are fused into a single unit which the Bible calls "one flesh." Intimacy means into me see. Couples must be able to see into each other's needs and wants – not try to play God's role of recreating and sanctifying their mate, but to have empathy and cover each the other's weaknesses.

In intimacy, habits are exposed. Telling signs will surface through observing whether your partner loves the bed (when and if they hold down jobs); do they listen to worldly music? A steady diet of violence on television or in the movies can anesthetize to pain and suffering? Do you like cooking and cleaning? Singles may feel they have a choice in these issues, but your choices after marriage will affect your mate.

A woman who was used to certain habits and ways of being before relationship now has to incorporate and accommodate her mate's and later their children's habits and ways of being. She will experience discomfort, a lack of **synergy**, as she tries to find her way from the way she was to the way she is becoming as part of a couple and family unit. She may grieve the old ways (lack of privacy, new accountability, etc.), if she enjoyed them or she may rejoice in the new ways, depending on her level of commitment to Christ, to the marriage, and her level of self-esteem. Some things must be relinquished, some things must be embraced; and still others she will not want to compromise. How to keep her sense of self while embracing others will be a big challenge that must be overcome.

CHAPTER V

Releasing the Anointing to Become a Force for God Through Accepting His Divine Authority

"Fear of the LORD is the beginning of knowledge.
Only fools despise wisdom and discipline." Proverbs 1:7.

Who is God? What we come to believe about God will determine how we live our lives and how we treat others. Our answer to this most important question will determine whether we seek to live open before Him or seek to live in hiding from Him. What you believe about who God is will determine how you respond to both blessings and adversity. In trouble, you will turn to God for strength and comfort or turn away in bitterness and anger. In times of blessings, you will give God thanks or give yourself credit. What you believe about God will determine where you spend eternity.

I have many testimonies of God's interventions and mercy in my life. Through prayer and meditation, I have chosen this one to share with my readers.

One day I got up early and wrote out a list of about eight things to do. First on the list was to head to Ft. Bragg in Fayetteville to take care of some VA things. Next, I drove back to Aberdeen where I would take care of a small bill that we'd incurred before the recent death of my husband. I knew from experience that small things can get out of hand if they aren't handled quickly.

After paying this bill, I found that my car had a flat tire. For some reason, I became livid with anger! It was a small thing, but for some reason, it unleashed an avalanche of emotions in me. All I could think about was I still have several things left on my agenda to do! I don't have time for this! I looked at my watch. Then I decided to try to drive the car the short distance to the nearby service station, but I could not. The noise beneath the car let me know I was messing up the rim. So I stopped the car, got out in the hot sun and walked the 10 minutes to the service station. Even though it was a short distance, under the sweltering sun I was drenched with sweat by the time I arrived at the station. I was even more irritated!

I called my senior pastor and told him my situation. On my agenda, I was scheduled to meet him at the church and go serve communion to our sick and shut in. He calmed my nerves, and promised to pick me up after his last counseling session.

When pastor arrived, I left my car key and cell phone number with instructions for the attendant who promised to get in touch with me when the tire was repaired. Then he warned me there would be a road charge, even though the car was within walking distance.

Well, the rest of day went quickly. I checked my cell phone. I had received no call from the attendant and I did not get an answer when I attempted to call. There was nothing left to do but return to the station. Even before we turned in to the lot, I knew the service station closed.

"Why hadn't they called me!!! Pastor looked helpless; I was really upset. I'd allowed myself to temporarily forget about the car as I'd gotten lost in ministering to the sick and shut-in. Because he had a part-time evening job, pastor had to leave me at the station. I assured him I would be just fine. I settled down on the outside bench and waited for my sister to pick me up. She had a 30-minute drive.

After a while of sitting there, I became aware of a black car that was parked just outside of my right peripheral vision - only a few feet away. In my irritation and preoccupation with self, I had failed to notice it before.

Now, a young lady got out and went to the back of the car and opened the trunk. As she placed her purse inside, she asked me, "Are you waiting on someone?" I was still miffed and didn't feel like talking, so I said, "Yes," rather stiffly. She tried again, "Do you have a car here?" Another one word answer, "Yes!" What she said next was music to my ears. "I can help you get your car; I'm the night auditor." Boy! Did my attitude change! I brightened up and said sincerely, "Thank you so very much!" I jumped up from that bench, watched her put the key in the door and briskly followed her inside. I could feel the tension in me disappearing. I was sincerely sorry I had been so ill; it wasn't her fault.

Once inside, she went around the counter and picked up the phone to call the owner. While she was talking, she reached in the drawer and soon retrieved my service ticket. I could see my car keys hanging on the wall behind her.

She hung up, told me my charge and started to ring up my bill. Suddenly she broke down and started crying. I stood still and waited for her to stop. Finally, she sniffled and said, "I guess you think I'm crazy, don't you?" I said, "No, I think you're hurting." I continued, "You just happen to be talking to a minister." At this, she started to cry even harder. Like before, I waited patiently, saying nothing. I waved through the window for my sister to go on back.

When she stopped crying, I hugged her and prepared to listen. She told me the most incredible story about the difficulties she was going through in a marriage to a drug addicted spouse. I was able to share my story of faith and victory with trust in Christ, and pray with her. I also gave her a manuscript copy of "Women are Spiritual BRIDGES," to read.

Several months later, I received a Christmas card from her saying, I "had been the guardian angel she had been praying for." She revealed that she had been sitting in that car planning to commit suicide! My story was helping her to cope better. They had started back to church.

I was glad God had interrupted my day. I don't want to die old, I want to die God-used! From then on, I began to be open to the guiding of the Spirit of God. My daily schedules are flexible now as I look for opportunities to share with whosoever the power of God in my life.

In Matthew 5:13 Jesus tells us we are the salt of the earth, but if salt loses its flavor it is not good for anything. All of life is tasteless and tedious without love. Even acts of generosity that is done out of obligation, but without sincere love, leave us empty and unfulfilled. Love represents the salt. It is the energy and the flavor of our lives.

Every day can be exciting if we see ourselves as God's ambassadors or secret agents, waiting for opportunities to sprinkle some salt on the tasteless lives of the people we encounter. For example, never miss another time to tell someone they look nice, or you like the way they are wearing their hair. Don't be afraid to ask for help from someone when there is a need. The other person may get tremendous satisfaction when it is done in the right way. Simple comments can add flavor to someone's day.

Loving others takes effort, and sometimes we allow ourselves to become careless or lazy in dispensing this gift. I hope you will actively express God's love everywhere you go, sprinkling salt on everyone you meet because God has placed you where you are for that very purpose. Can He trust you to have ears to hear and eyes to see where the Spirit of the Lord is leading?

Going beyond knowledge to Personal Relationship

"That which is born of the flesh is flesh, and that which is born of the Spirit is spirit."
Do not be amazed that I said to you, 'You must be born again.' John 3:7

In this age of information, knowledge is plentiful, but wisdom is scarce. Wisdom is the ability to see life from God's perspective and then to know the best course of action to take. Wisdom means far more than simply knowing a lot. It means using that "knowing" to safely navigate your way through life. Another name for wisdom is discernment. Discernment is a basic attitude of judging all things that affects every area of a believer's life as good or bad.

The foundation of knowledge is to fear the LORD—to honor and respect God, to live in awe of His power, and to obey His Word. Faith in God should be the controlling principle for understanding the world, understanding your attitude, and understanding why you act the way you do.

"….Christ the power of God and the wisdom of God." 1 Corinthians 1:24

We can gain access to God's wisdom only through making God's Son, Jesus the Christ, the LORD and Master of our life. For no man comes to the Father except through the Son. (John 14:6) Jesus said "I am the way, the truth and the life." How much there is in the Name of Jesus! Once we accept Salvation, God's anointing is released in our lives. The anointing breaks yokes and sets the captives free.

Sometimes when one is seeking a favor, a friend may direct you to someone else and say, "When you see him, mention my name." The use of a name may mean a good position to you, it may get you some special favor; it may even reprieve a death sentence. But a human name has limits. It does not go beyond the human sphere. No name of any human creature has any special weight with God. He honors fully only one Name – the Name of His Son Jesus. No body is beyond the reach of that Name. All creatures acknowledge the power of that Name. You must develop the mind of Christ in order to choose the right decisions and be able to obey His Word. You can only gain access to the mind of Christ by accepting all of Him. As you obey, God will use His power in your favor.

Says Peter to the men of Israel: "His Name through faith in His Name hath made this man strong" (Acts 3:16). All blessing is found in that Name, and faith releases that power for our benefit. Even in this world one must have authorization to use another's name. Christ never gave His Name to sinners to use, unless first the sinner has believed on His Name, and thus has become a child of God (John 1:12). After that, there are untold blessings available for the believer in the Name of Jesus. Once you accept His Son, you can have access to all the Father's blessings; there comes the indwelling of the Holy Spirit to help you mature spiritually.

> *If you declare with your mouth, "Jesus is Lord," and believe in your heart that God*
> *raised him from the dead, you will be saved. For it is with your heart that you*
> *believe and are justified, and it is with your mouth that you profess your faith*
> *and are saved."* Romans 10:9-10

The Word will cause you to settle down, stop arguing with God and humble yourself! The Word will instruct you on the proper way to live and treat others! The Word will also cause your position to change from wanting to lead to being led by the Holy Spirit. The Word will give you second sight by opening the eyes of your understanding. As you develop the mind of Christ, your faith will grow into unshakable faith. Unshakable faith will always find a way. You cannot depend on someone else's knowledge and understanding along the way – although good mentors are great to have. The Bible is God's word. And the Word became flesh and dwelt among us. Jesus is that Word. He loves you and will guide you through the person of the Holy Spirit. God is ready to assume full responsibility for the life totally yielded to Him. If you are ready to authorize God to become Head and Master of your life, all you need to do is believe and pray this simple prayer.

"Dear Heavenly Father, I come before you now confessing that I am a sinner. I repent of my sins and ask you to forgive me. I believe in my heart that Jesus the Christ is Your Son; that He died and you raised Him from the dead. I believe He is now seated at Your right hand interceding on my behalf. I confess that I want Jesus to come into my heart and be my LORD and Master. I believe that through His shed blood, I have eternal life. Please come into my heart and fill me with Your Holy Spirit power. I pray this prayer in Jesus name, Amen."

If you sincerely prayed this prayer, then according to Scripture you are saved! You are authorized and equipped. You now have the blood of Jesus, the righteousness of God, the New Testament and the Holy Spirit inside you to continually tell you what Jesus is saying and to give you God's commands. You have His Name to authorize you, and the Father dwelling in you, to do the works that living on this earth and in harmonious relationships demand.

Accept it; join a good Bible-based church and get to work serving the LORD through all of your relationships while you patiently wait on that special someone. And remember, God is working on that special someone that will eventually come into your life. In the meantime, will you be ready to both recognize and receive them? After all, the same God that speaks to you should be the same God that speaks to them and allows them to recognize the treasure in you.

How God's Authority Works

"Believe Me that I am in the Father, and the Father in Me. The words that I speak unto you I speak not of Myself: but the Father that dwells in Me, He doeth the works. He that believes in Me, the works that I do shall he do also; and greater works than these shall he do, because I go unto My Father." John 14: 11,-12

Notice according to those verses, Jesus followed what, in military terms, is called "a chain of command." Just as a general gives commands to the soldiers under him and then backs those commands with his authority, the Father told Jesus what to say and He said it. The Father told Him what to do and He did it. Then the Father dwelling in Him did the works. He backed Jesus up with His power and did things through Him that are humanly impossible.

That's the way God's system has always worked. Think again about Moses and the miracle at the Red Sea. What happened there? God gave Moses words to speak. He said "Tell the people to go forward." He also gave Moses a command to obey. "Stretch forth your rod and divide the sea." When Moses said what God said and did what He commanded, the Father did the work. He backed him up.

The same thing happened to Joshua. God gave him words to say and commands to obey. When Joshua said those words and acted on those commands, God backed him up, and he kept winning one impossible battle after another.

It's a simple process, and we can all operate in it. But to do so, we must believe. We must have faith in God. Since faith comes by hearing the WORD of God (Romans 10:17), that means we have to do what Joshua did and make that WORD the priority and final authority in our lives, meditating on it and speaking it all the time.

When you are facing battles that appear to be impossible to win, your natural mind will stagger. Your physical senses will try to talk you out of obeying God's command. The circumstances won't look right. Your emotions won't feel right. Pride will rise up; Anger and Grief will raise their two cents worth. People will tell you not to take it, and Satan will come to steal that command out of your heart and try to get you to do and say what he says instead of what God says.

In hard times as well as in good times, you must remember that you are a soldier in God's army. Remain humbly attuned to His voice. He will show Himself strong; always working behind the scenes on your behalf.

Stand still until He tells you to go. Open your mouth when He tells you to; close it when He tells you to; do exactly what the WORD has been teaching you. The WORD has been preparing you for battle. Psalm 119:67-68 teaches us that affliction is good for us because it teaches us to stay with God's Word and not go astray.

> *"For the LORD gives wisdom, and from His mouth comes knowledge and understanding. He stores up sound wisdom for the upright; He is a shield for those who walk in integrity, guarding the paths of justice, and He preserves the way of His godly ones."* Proverbs 2:6-7

Now that we know God and His Word, we are obligated to walk in it. You understand that those whom God loves, He changes. He does this thru hearing the Word, thru people and thru circumstances. You will become a people-changer and a history maker thru allowing God to use you. That is an awesome responsibility. But always remember that God will never send you to a place or allow you to deal with a situation without His power and Presence to preserve you.

Never doubt that God hears your prayers; but sin grieves His heart. All of heaven rejoices over saved souls. God has equipped you with everything you need to follow Him. Do not allow people and circumstances to weaken your faith in God's ability to see you through. Those that dig a pit for you, God promises will fall into it themselves. Even when He is silent, He is there. Keep on praising His name no matter what it looks like.

"But as it is written, "No eye has seen, no ear has heard, and no mind has imagined
the things that God has prepared for those who love him." 1 Corinthians 2:9

You have no way of fathoming the far reaching blessings that are available to your spouse, your children and their spouses and your grands and great-grands. All because you made the wise decision to follow Jesus and be a good soldier in the Army of the LORD!

Heeding Our Inward Witness

"Howbeit when He, the Spirit of truth, is come, He will guide you into all truth:
for He shall not speak of himself; but whatsoever He shall hear, that shall He speak:
and He will shew you things to come." John 16:3

If God approached you at this moment, and asked what you wanted from Him, what would you ask of Him? When given a chance to have anything in this world, Solomon asked for wisdom (1 Kings 3:1-28) - "an understanding mind" - in order to lead well and to make right decisions. We can also ask God for this same wisdom (James 1:5) in whatever walk of life we find ourselves in.

Notice that Solomon asked for discernment to carry out his job, he did not ask God to do the job for him. WE SHOULD NOT ASK GOD TO DO FOR US WHAT HE WANTS TO DO THROUGH US. Instead, we should ask God to give us the wisdom to know what to do and the strength and courage to follow through on it. When it comes to choosing our lifetime companion, many may capture our attention, but only one should be qualified of God to capture our heart. How will you be able to correctly discern that this is the one out of many?

> *"That the God of our LORD Jesus Christ, the Father of glory, may give unto you the Spirit of wisdom and revelation in the knowledge of Him; the eyes of your understanding being opened ..."* Ephesians 1:17-18

Using Godly wisdom is your ability to understand yourself as well as others and to correctly discern situations you are in.

From Titus chapter 2 and verse 12, we are instructed to "deny ungodliness and worldly lust, and to live soberly, righteously, and godly in this present world." **Godly Wisdom then is your ability to make the choices necessary to create the most favorable outcomes for everyone involved in every situation we find ourselves in.**

True Godly wisdom gives you authority to transcend this life. If you obey God you will:

Know when you are in a potentially harmful situation

Know when you can say or do something to turn a situation in your favor

Understand choices that will increase your knowledge and happiness

Better understand why people make the decisions they make

Gain the favor and influence of other people

Gain insight into an otherwise unknown thing to you

Understand that failure and success are equally important in life

Keep your body and mind in a healthy state through proper decision making

Know when it is best to be still and keep quiet as God works behind the scenes

Seeing into the heart of people and how to pray for them

These are just a few of the things Godly wisdom can do to help you live the abundant life Christ promises you. By being discerning, we will take the time to carefully weigh out and make wise decisions. You will be amazed at what making a few wise choices will do to turn things around in your life. Remember, the wise decision is very often the most difficult and sometimes does not seem to be the most beneficial at the time.

There are many major life decisions that using godly wisdom is very useful for; as well as many day to day and smaller scale situations where the use of Godly wisdom will keep your life headed in a positive direction. Here are some of the major and not so major situations where wisdom should be used.

Choosing a lifetime companion
Getting an education
Deciding which career to pursue
Deciding to have a family
Deciding to begin your own company
The handling of the death of a loved one
Talking to someone who has given up on life

CHAPTER VI

Effects of Personal Reasoning on Relationships

Is Romantic Love Strong Enough to Sustain a Relationship?

"Come, Let us Reason together, says the LORD..." Isaiah 1:18

Most people in modern society would not marry each other were they not in the throes of romantic love. This emotion is so intense until it is often thought of as "true love" and recognized as the sole reason to marry or even stay married to each other. There is this bizarre lack of knowledge as to what causes intense feelings between two people in the first place. This is a profound ignorance!

Let's take a look at one case. She loved him so much when she married him eight years ago. Because of the intense feelings he had for her, he knew that keeping his vows to her would be easy. He felt he would always love her. Now, they are getting a divorce. He says he no longer "feels" the way he used to. She says the same thing. Neither one seems to have a clear answer of why but they both realize that their love for one another has "died." Some statistics say that romantic love only last an average of three to four years.

If only they had a sign "Abandon reason all you who enter here" over the door of the divorce courts of our country. What we need to make a relationship work is a thorough knowledge of how our emotions work and why intensity does not guarantee longevity. David Burns in "Feeling Good" (1980) states that emotions follow thoughts like a baby duck follows their mother. However, just because they follow their mother does not mean that the mother knows where she is going. As Jesus inferred, thoughts produce emotions. Therefore, if we are going to understand the romantic love emotion, we had better understand the "thinking" behind it.

Romantic love is caused by an evaluation of the love interest. It is the result of a person reasoning and telling themselves over and over again how wonderful the traits of this other person are (real or imagined) and what a great mate they will make. The negative traits are ignored. It is a conditional love. It exists all too often because one or both parties believe that the other is nearly perfect.

After being with someone day and night and seeing that they are not as perfect as we thought – the evaluations begin to change. The intensity of the love emotion begins to diminish because of the change in our evaluations. Day to day living, watching the person forget something we asked them to do; listening to them snore; going into the bathroom and smelling the remains of their use, etc. If we are not careful, we may end up hating the other person with the same intensity that we once "loved" them. Since it is such a terminating process, romantic love is a poor thing to base a marriage on. Other areas of compatibility between two people are more significant.

The philosophy of life of the other person is a better indication of how they will behave in an intimate stressful relationship like marriage. What is a philosophy of life? It is a set of beliefs that we use to determine how we react to and interact with our environment.

One way to predict whether a relationship will work out is to see how the beloved treats their enemies. Inevitably in an on-going relationship like marriage, we are going to "cross" the other person. If they rant and rave about their enemies and don't see their part in helping to bring about crisis with others – they won't be kind to you when you cross them (even though accidentally). How are their problem-solving skills? Do they place blame or do they seek to solve problems? Are they flexible or are they rigid and demanding? Do they learn from their mistakes or seek the advice of worthy mentors?

Everybody has something they want from a relationship. Are they willing to discuss these desires and try and fill some of them? Are they the center of the universe – only thinking about their own desires? People that are "nice" to others because they understand the human plight are much easier to get along with than overly opinionated, critical people. If they only have negative things to say about others, especially ex-relationships, that is not a good sign.

Are they overly apologetic? Do they accept themselves? People will often treat you like they treat themselves. If they are obsessed with themselves even negatively, they may not be mentally healthy enough to love another. Be careful about people who think you will complete them. Usually they will only finish you off!

Examine Your Childhood Experiences

"For as he thinks in his heart …" Proverbs 23:7

Have you ever tried to hold a 2–3 month old baby close to you? You can tell a lot about how that child is being oriented to its world. If the child snuggles – becomes soft and molds itself to your body, it is trusting and feels safe. If the child's back stiffens and it refuses to become pliable and snuggle close, it is being raised in a less than comfortable environment. The child is learning not to trust its world and does not feel safe. How does this child's world look? In a phrase, threatening and confusing.

Over time, there is fear of rejection; a lack of bonding which translates into the child's clinging to its caretaker but refusing others. This child may be exposed to a steady diet of loud music and the television is its mechanical babysitter. There are rude "suddenlys" in the child's life such as bursts of shouting, cursing and being rudely shoved or tossed around. The child learns to be tense, hyper vigilant – like a shell shot soldier. Although it is unable to protect itself, this child is constantly at attention and looking out for the "enemy" as evidenced in the stiffness of its countenance.

Without intervention, this child will grow up to be fearful and distrust; it will have a warped view of the world as a dangerous and confusing place. Their beliefs will guide their actions.

A Mindset of Extremes

As an adult, the inability to trust and feel safe is ingrained in a child raised in an unpredictable and uncomfortable environment which will translate in to a mindset of extremes. Either this child grows up to believe they are lower than other human beings or superior to others. Hence such statements as, "I can do badly all by myself," is adopted. This child will have a difficult time making and maintaining friends – much less being intimate with another person.

An adult who has been raised in an abusive and chaotic world may show signs in their facial expression. They may have a flat affect, always scanning their environment for perceived danger; seldom smiling and be unable to see the humor in funny situations. They will take the opposite view in an issue in order to push the limits; and may jump to conclusions – cutting in on a speaker because they already know what they are going to say.

They are territorial to the point of marking their things and their area; and have a hard time sharing. This type of person may walk around on egg shells and refuse to use their voice because of being "beaten" into passivity. Or they may be loud and use "just joking" as a means of getting their point across. Peacekeeping techniques, such as open communications, appear boring and a waste of time.

Their outlook on life is negative. They will not trust anyone with their true feelings for fear of ridicule or being deceived. Out of a sense of disillusionment, they will question the validity of God's Word. This individual may feel a sense of entitlement, "The world owes me." Their dress may be extreme or overly modest. The bottom line is that people raised from childhood in uncertain, chaotic or dysfunctional households, will be persons of extremes and find it hard to strike a balance. They will be unable to sympathize because of having gotten use to a steady diet of suffering and blood shed. They are generally very needy or display a toughness that says "I don't need anybody!"

Beware if you were raised in a chaotic households or a war zone. You will unconsciously try to find someone who likes to argue and be at odds because your idea of how love is shown is twisted by that early learning model. You will not feel comfortable with peace and overlook a person with a quiet spirit as weak or someone to be manipulated and dominated.

Early Role Models

Take your father as your first role model for example. Whether present or absent, he was your first role model. If he was present, then it will be more obvious that his habits, attitudes, language (ways of expressing himself) are making an impact on you – whether you chose to look for a companion like your father or whether you chose to look for the opposite, he is your first role model. Even if he was absent from the home, he provided that role model (a longing to know what he was like and if all that Mama told you about him was correct). After examining this model, go through your mind and search out the effects of every other male model – from brothers and uncles to teachers and preachers. All have had an impact on how you perceive men should be in relationship.

Next, take a look at the type of home you were raised in. If it was female dominated, you will pick up – unconsciously the habits of being dominant in relationship – even if you've learned better through watching what happened in these relationships. There are subtle nuances and ways of being that can only be learned through childhood upbringing - from body language to "tongue needs to be put in check." Because they are subtle, you may not know they are operating in your life until after you are already in relationship. Most males, worth their salt, may initially be attracted to you perhaps because of looks, etc., but just because you qualify for their attention, they will quickly find out that you do not qualify for their heart if the fruit of the spirit is not at work in you.

As a woman of God, you must be able to "Be still" in the midst of the storm, trust God and know He will bless Godly efforts on your behalf. In this effort, discernment and patience will be your most important allies.

While you wait, ask yourself "Are my thoughts and my feelings in line with a particular point of view. Or are they in line with what God's feelings are about this situation?" Sometimes our own emotions get in the way of our being able to think objectively. In our zeal to "save someone from the pain we've endured, we say or do the wrong thing. We talk instead of listening. We fret instead of praying. We do and try to fix it on our own rather than trusting God to do what He says He will do.

"Being still" isn't easy for a human woman because we may have been so programmed with the ways of the world and listening to the bitter comments of unfulfilled women as we grew up. We may have unconsciously adopted her ways; unconsciously accepted that all men are "bad, cursed of God and no good." If we are not careful, we will set up committees in our heads that will look to confirm these thoughts in every potential mate we meet.

However, there are exceptions; you are not required to stay with an individual who may produce emotional or physical damage to health and welfare or one who tries to coerce you into illegal or immoral activities which are against the laws of man and the Word of God.

Be careful woman of God. Look to your own background before becoming a part of a committed relationship. Without Godly discernment, whatever committees are operating in your mind may allow you to sabotage every relationship. Somehow, your mind and body may believe that you are incomplete without a mate, and lead you into all kinds of disastrous affairs. These early background experiences may trip you up; cause a lack of clarity and even confusion when coming to the most important decision of who will finally become your lifetime companion. Let me explain.

It is a natural response to be attracted to the opposite sex, based on how you experienced them (and observed them in relationship), in the household in which you grew up in. It will also be natural for you to unconsciously copy this model in your own relationship, regardless of whether it was good or bad, it's the only role model you had. You either chose to embrace or choose to reject that model, but it is basic to your final decision.

Either way, it's important for you to understand, however you have been shaped by your experiences, you will draw unto yourself your like opposite. This means whatever qualities you possess – good or bad, the universe will draw a person into your life that possesses these same qualities. [More to come on the Law of Attraction.]

Your greatest task will be to find someone who is willing to cooperate with your already preconceived ideas of how relationship should work with you. In other words, "It's your world; you must try to fit someone else into it." [Tongue in cheek, of course.]

Pray that those ideas line up with the Word of God. A woman of God must know her place is beside her husband, not under him, over him and certainly not in front of him.

For instance, if you are a woman with a quiet spirit who loves to read and your idea of a terrific evening is curling up on the sofa with a good book or a romantic television program or movie, and your spouse is someone who loves a rip roaring western or a sports enthusiasts; neither of these things are wrong, but you will need to learn how to fit into each other's lifestyle and remain absolutely neutral where right and wrong are concerned. Each should want the other to be happy and contented and not try to force the other to change, unless his behavior is life threatening or criminal. Just be a Godly example. Nothing makes one so miserable as to have the other try to recreate whom God has created them to be.

Don't Take His Manhood

> *"But the wisdom that comes from heaven is first of all pure; then peace-loving,*
> *considerate, submissive, full of mercy and good fruit, impartial and sincere."*
> (James 3:17)

Most women want a man of authority, one they can respect and look up to. One who will earn a living and take care of what needs repairing in the home; but she does not want him to necessarily take charge when it comes to important decisions – such as how his paycheck will be spent or how the children should be disciplined. Suddenly, she rises up and decides that she will be in charge. She gets out of the role of a submissive wife and is ready to use whatever weapons are necessary to get her way. She may throw a temper tantrum, scream; call him less than a man and talk about his lack of performance in bed. They bump heads and she wonders why things are not working. The battle scars she has inflicted while invisible will be long lasting as she watches affection and interest in her fly out the window. Either he is the man she was attracted to – or he wasn't. A battle of wills ensues and as it progresses, his actions or lack thereof, will determine whether they are able to live in peace together.

The fact of the matter is if he buckles under to her demanding ways, she will lose respect for him. If he does not buckle under to her, she will find herself at odds in a competition that she really will not be happy winning.

Take Eve for instance, I can imagine that if Adam had not buckled under to eating that fruit, Eve would probably have nagged him to death for the rest of their eternal life – unless God stepped in of course. After sinning, Adam's nature changed to one of dominance; and Eve's to focusing on pleasing Him and losing her identity. She could no longer be in harmony with Adam for *how can two walk together unless they agree?* (Amos 3:3) Therefore, Adam, like many men after him, had to choose whether to please God or please that woman. Better to remember that a mate is not God; they are human and in process just as you are. Also remember, you are not his mother and he is not your child or grandchild! He does not need you to elevate yourself by pointing out his every weakness. You are to cover them!

How spiritually mature love is MANIFESTED: One of the marks of immaturity as seen in babies is an utter preoccupation with self. Paul, after explaining that he had put away childish things, goes on to show that "Love is patient, love is kind. It does not envy, it does not boast, it is not proud. It is not rude, IT IS NOT SELF-SEEKING, it is not easily angered, it keeps no record of wrongs. Love does not delight in evil but rejoices with the truth. It always protects, always trusts, always hopes, always perseveres. LOVE NEVER FAILS …" (1Corinthians 13:4–8).

So the trajectory from immaturity to maturity leads outward from self. Mature love is selfless love. Immature love is self-love.

Furthermore, Paul goes on to explain that no matter what else we can do – speak in angelic or human tongues we didn't learn, demonstrate the gift of prophecy, fathom mysteries like Daniel did, or even exercise mountain-moving faith – if we can't express love, spiritually we're nothing. Appropriate, godly love then is at the heart of spiritual maturity. Knowing that, isn't it something we ought to be actively seeking to achieve and express?

Love is the first listed fruit of the Holy Spirit (Galatians 5:22). I believe the fruit are listed in an order; you can't have the others without first having love. As Paul also taught, every Christian should

"Follow the way of love …" (1Corinthians 14:1).

When Paul describes to the Corinthian congregation the ways in which godly love is manifested, he is providing a treatise on spiritual maturity. Spiritual maturity is characterized by patience, good manners (civility), lack of envy, humility and a temper that is well under control. The spiritually mature person is not preoccupied with himself or herself. He or she has died to self.

Those who have reached a high level of spiritual maturity are no longer interested in keeping track of other people's mistakes, sins and faults (1Corinthians 13:5). As Paul puts it, "they keep no record of wrongs." They have no war chest of offenses to unload on those over whom they wish to gain a psychological advantage in an argument. A mature Christian rejoices in every new discovery of truth. He or she actively seeks out truth and follows it wherever it leads. He is not ashamed to jettison old errors in favor of better understanding.

Those who have reached higher plains of maturity take no delight – vicariously or otherwise – in evil. They do not view other's evil as a way of making themselves look good by contrast. (One of the standard techniques of an emotionally immature person is to provoke another person to anger, and then attack them for the anger. This perfectly reflects the mind of Satan.)

A spiritually mature person has no wish to participate in evil, and they don't delight in, or take advantage of it when others fall into sin. They have no appetite for scandal. They take no delight in plotting evil, living vicariously in the evil of others, or in hearing about the evil that men do. They actively seek to drive back the toxic spiritual darkness that envelops this world. Those who are spiritually mature seek to protect others who are vulnerable in a dangerous world. Just as Jesus said to Peter:

> *"Simon, Simon, Satan has asked to sift you as wheat. BUT I HAVE*
> *PRAYED FOR YOU, Simon, that your faith may not fail ..."*
> (Luke 22:31-32)

Mature Christians spend much time in intercessory prayer for others (Luke 22:31; 1Thessalonians 5:17). They are more focused on the needs of others than themselves. Those who are spiritually advanced are not paranoid. They "**believe all things**" and offer others the benefit of the doubt. They are not fearful and suspicious, always expecting the worst (1Corinthians 13:7).

A person who loves, hangs in there and perseveres. He or she has hope and is optimistic about what God has in store for his faithful children. Mature Christians are not "fair weather friends." They stick with you in your worst as well as your best moments.

One of the most important characteristics of mature Christian love is that it "**never fails**" (1Corinthians 13:8). Like the love of God itself, it is constant, unwavering, always there. A fully mature Christian has achieved a steady state of love. This kind of love is far greater than either faith or hope. It is the most concrete expression of spiritual maturity there is. Just as God never gives up on us (Philippians 1:6), We must learn not to give up on each other. We are not called to reject someone simply because we disagree on a point of doctrine, or an interpretation of facts or acts.

Spiritual maturity also involves sensitivity to, and powerful leading by, the Holy Spirit. It is the Holy Spirit that gives us the capacity to love as God loves (as we learned earlier – Romans 5:5). The influence of the Spirit of God in a spiritually immature person is at best but a flickering ember. In the spiritually mature, it is a roaring flame. As we move deeper into obedience to God, the influence of the Holy Spirit grows greater.

As Peter said,

> *"We are witnesses of these things, and so is the Holy Spirit Whom*
> *God has given to those that obey him." (Acts 5:32)*

At the same time, it is the Holy Spirit that not only strengthens our faith but also enables us to more fully comprehend and be filled with God's love. The apostle Paul prayed:

"I pray that out of his glorious riches he may strengthen you with power through his Spirit in your inner being, so that Christ may dwell in your hearts through faith. And I pray that you, being rooted and established in love, may have power, together with all the saints, to grasp how wide and long and high and deep is the love of Christ, and to know this love that surpasses knowledge — that you may be filled to the measure of all the fullness of God." Ephesians 3:16-19

The Holy Spirit imparts the power of God to the people of God (Acts 1:8). It enables us to transcend our natural human capacities and limitations. The more of God's Spirit we have indwelling, the quicker we'll attain to spiritual maturity. Since the capacity to love, in a godly way is a product of the Holy Spirit, so spiritual maturity is also its fruit.

When it comes to submission, the Holy Spirit led woman will understand submission means standing beside and not under. She must never forget her vows to love sacrificially. At stressful times, the first words out of her mouth should be "Let's pray about this," therefore, turning the focus onto God's ever present help in the time of a storm.

Role Dominance

There are some unspoken agreements in a marriage relationship that cannot be discussed beforehand. One of these is role dominance. This is because role dominance can only be detected and played out in intimate relationship. It is an archetype that will surface, like Cool Aid becoming Cool Aid only when all of the ingredients are added together. If one of the ingredients is missing, it's not Cool Aid! Similarly, your unique personality and ways of being will surface only when you try living in another's unique personality and ways of being.

In healthy relationships, leadership is shared and goes back and forth among couples most of the time without notice. No one is a dictator--leading is by consensus. Whoever is most qualified in a particular area emerges as the leader for that particular situation. If leadership does not flow freely back and forth, the relationship becomes unbalanced. Couples should be good friends who respect each other first. "Good" friends often share leadership without even realizing it. They understand give and take is a part of life.

We have all been in relationships where we felt we were giving, and getting little in return. How long was it before the relationship ended once we started thinking we were being used? But, that's what happens when someone takes more than they give in a relationship. Look at our divorce statistics and you will see that this statement is true.

How do you know if you are giving the other person what they want? When all else fails, **ask**. Do the little things. Make note of a person's Birthday and send them a card. Plan a special evening where both enjoy a concert, a play a wholesome movie together. Do something together. Reward positive behavior by statements like, "It was nice of you to send the card." Etc… We can be detectives to find out other's likes and dislikes. These and other positive steps help build relationships. Above all be creative. But don't just be, do something!

Beware: Familiarity May Breed Contempt

"Don't pick on people, jump on their failures, and criticize their faults— unless, of course, you want the same treatment. That critical spirit has a way of boomeranging. It's easy to see a smudge on your neighbor's face and be oblivious to the ugly sneer on your own. Do you have the nerve to say, 'Let me wash your face for you,' when your own face is distorted by contempt? It's this whole traveling road-show mentality all over again, playing a holier-than-thou part instead of just living your part. Wipe that ugly sneer off your own face, and you might be fit to offer a washcloth to your neighbor." (Matthew 7:1-5, the Message)

The question is often asked why people who get married have less of a chance of staying together than those who live together – even for years. I don't know if you will get a clear cut answer for this, but I suspect marriage gives the parties involved a false sense of owning each other. Before marriage, there is no commitment because there is no public declaration before God and man. After marriage parties think they own one another rather than understanding they have made vows to each other and to God. Whether they realize God is part of the union and should be consulted in decision-making makes a difference in how they treat one another. Either way, whether both hearts are regenerate (saved) or one or both are unregenerate (unsaved) will make a difference in whether the relationship stands a chance of enduring.

Because "All have sinned and come short of the glory of God," seeing the other's faults will surface pretty quickly with close proximity. Even men and women of God may soon become disappointed as they see the other without rose colored glasses. A regenerated heart is a grateful heart that knows only God can "fix" another human to be what He wants it to be. An unregenerate heart will find fault, forgetting that she is not perfect and needs to see the beam in her own eye before being able to see clearly the faults in another. Murmuring and complaining always brings wrath and judgment from God. It will bring the same from your partner. We are told to do everything without grumbling or complaining. (Phil. 2:14) In other words, can you see my faults and weaknesses and still love me? Or do I have to give up me(the one whom God is creating me to be) to be loved by you?

A regenerate heart will pray for her spouse and use the words of the Serenity prayer *"God Grant me Serenity to accept the things I cannot change; the Courage to change the things I can, and the Wisdom to know the difference,"* as she refers wisely to praying that her mate will accept kindly whatever faults he finds in her.

CHAPTER VII

Dating and Marriage God's Way

Before we can discuss what to look for in a suitable spouse, we need to be able to recognize what issues are involved in forming a whole and healthy relationship. To begin with, ask yourself,

Is God a matchmaker?

"GOD said, "It's not good for the Man to be alone; I'll make him <u>a helper, a companion</u>." So GOD formed from the dirt of the ground all the animals of the field and all the birds of the air. He brought them to the Man to see what he would name them. Whatever the Man called each living creature that was its name. The Man named the cattle, named the birds of the air, named the wild animals; but he didn't find a suitable companion. GOD put the Man into a deep sleep. As he slept he removed one of his ribs and replaced it with flesh. GOD then used the rib that he had taken from the Man to make Woman and presented her to the Man. The Man said, "Finally! Bone of my bone, flesh of my flesh! Name her Woman for she was made from Man." Therefore *a man leaves his father and mother and embraces his wife. They become one flesh. The two of them, the Man and his Wife, were naked, but they felt no shame.* "(*Genesis 2:18-25*).

This was the first marriage; a marriage God approved of. Marriage existed before sin. God fashioned Adam a mate, so does God have a particular person chosen to be your spouse? The idea that He does has been used for years to comfort frustrated Christians who worry that they'll never find their lifetime companion; and given that we believe God to be all-knowing and all-powerful, there is a certain amount of comfort in thinking that He's got somebody picked out for us all.

But if you think about that idea for a while, some questions and problems present themselves. If God has somebody "picked out" for you, should you actively search for said person, or trust that God will bring them into your life? How will you recognize that said somebody is "the one"?

And what about the gift of singleness? Not everyone is destined to get married. Does our society frown upon the unmarried, especially after they reach a certain age? Those who attempt to "hunt" for a mate out of God's order are in danger of getting into unfulfilling and abusive relationships.

This may happen through the most popular media of our time – internet dating services. Men who are incarcerated have nothing but time on their hands. Many spend this time carving out a name and a sad story to bring out the nurturing instinct in lonely, unsuspecting women.

> *"But since sexual immorality is occurring, each man should have sexual relations with his own wife, and each woman with her own husband."* 1 Corinthians 7:2

First, [In 1 Corinthians,] Paul stops short of guaranteeing that God will provide a spouse to anyone who wants one. Neither here nor anywhere else does Paul—or any biblical writer—lock God into a required response to any human need. There is always the possibility that God will choose not to meet a need directly but to give the grace to live contentedly with unfulfilled desires, a point Paul stresses in his second letter to this church (2 Cor 12:7-10).

Still Paul puts emphasis on hope in his teaching on marriage, and throughout his writings urges us toward faith in a God who provides all of our needs in Jesus Christ (Phil 4:19). If you want to be married, you certainly have reason to stay hopeful that God will provide someone to meet that need unless He changes your desire or in some clear way shuts the door.

Again, it is important as you maintain this hope to keep your expectations within reasonable bounds. If you're thinking that God has one ideal choice for you, you may set your standards for that person impossibly high. When we consider the perspective on God's role which was in Paul's mind as he wrote 1 Corinthians 7, it seems to be not that God has one ideal person for you to marry—but that God will help you find a *suitable* companion. This is usually a more satisfying thought to dwell on.

Any person whom He gives you to marry will have imperfections and failings, just as you do. Still that person will complement you in a way that will work for your greater happiness and a more fruitful life together for Christ. Next, ask

What Does it Mean to Be a Helper

Here, the reader needs to refer back to what has already been expounded upon in Chapter one: "What God Meant."

> *In Eve, God provided a "suitable helper" (Genesis 2:20). Eve was suitable because she shared with Adam the image and likeness of God – the image that permits human beings to relate on every dimension of personality (emotional, intellectual, spiritual, physical, etc.). Only another being who, like Adam, was shaped in the image of God would be suitable.*

The word for "helper" here is 'ezer. It means "a help," "a support," "an assistant." Before we understand this concept to imply inferiority or subordination, we should note that the root is used in the Old Testament to speak of God as helper of His nation and of individuals. God is man's helper in all kinds of distress (Exodus 18:4; Deuteronomy 33:7, 26, 29; Psalms 20:2; 33:20; 70:5; 89:19; 115:9-11; 121:1; 124:8; 146:5; Hosea 13:9). We do not conclude from this that God is inferior to the person He helps. Then, neither should we refer to woman as being inferior to man. Rather,

1) A helper is one who provides Godly Wisdom to help her spouse and family navigate through this evil world.
2) A helper also provides encouragement to strengthen her spouse in times of battle (warfare).

3) A helper is one who rejoices with him and grieves with him as each case calls for. Now ask yourself,

What it Means to Be Evenly Yoked

How can an unregenerate (unsaved) heart advise of spiritual things? What does it mean to be __un__evenly yoked? What does it mean to possess a regenerate (saved) heart? What does it mean to be a suitable companion?

From 1 Corinthians 2:14-16 (The Message), "The unspiritual self, just as it is by nature, can't receive the gifts of God's Spirit. There's no capacity for them. They seem like so much silliness. Spirit can be known only by spirit—God's Spirit and our spirits in open communion. Spiritually alive, we have access to everything God's Spirit is doing, and can't be judged by unspiritual critics. Isaiah's question, *"Is there anyone around who knows God's Spirit, anyone who knows what He is doing?"* has been answered: Christ knows, and we have Christ's Spirit."

But God has revealed them to us by his Spirit: for the Spirit searches all things, yes, the deep things of God. For what man knows the things of a man, save the spirit of man which is in him? even so the things of God knows no man, but the Spirit of God. Now we have received, not the spirit of the world, but the spirit which is of God; that we might know the things that are freely given to us of God. ..." 1 Corinthians 2:10-12

If we are born again, we are warned at 2 Corinthians chapter six and verse fourteen, *"Be you not unequally yoked together with unbelievers: for what fellowship has righteousness with unrighteousness? And what communion has light with darkness?"*

Unbelievers are those who are unsaved and therefore, whose hearts have not been regenerated by Christ; while a regenerate heart is one that has accepted Christ and now possesses the Holy Spirit. The heart has been circumcised and is being transformed by God. If a believer marries an unbeliever, this spells disaster waiting to happen. There is no way for the two of them to clearly communicate, according to first Corinthians chapter two, verses fourteen through sixteen – one is living in darkness while the other is living in the light. Remember, if God has not yet been able to bend the will of another, no human being will be capable of doing it. If you believe your intended is really wheat that now seems to be a tare, time will be your greatest ally.

"Be ye not unevenly yoked with unbelievers; for what fellowship has righteousness with unrighteousness? And what communion has light with darkness?" (2 Corinthians 6:14-15)

The Bible strictly warns Christians over and over again not to be yoked to someone who has not fallen in Love with Jesus the way they have…. There is two kinds of wisdom that has been let loose in the world. **"…** *having been firmly rooted and now being built up in Him and established in your faith, just as you were instructed, and overflowing with gratitude. See to it that no one takes you captive through philosophy and empty deception, according to the tradition of men, according to the elementary principles of the world, rather than according to Christ."* Colossians 2:7-8

God's thoughts are not the world's thoughts. *"For my thoughts are not your thoughts, neither are your ways my ways," declares the LORD."* Isaiah 55:8 In other words, your thoughts are may be captured more like the world and your love ones thoughts may be captured more like God's thoughts.

There is only one Holy Spirit and His job is to make all true Christians think alike (1 Corinthians 12:13) by giving them the mind of Christ. *"…so that with one mind and one voice you may glorify the God and Father of our Lord Jesus Christ."* Romans 15:6 God wants believers to recognize each other all over the world and go to each other for protection. It is also to discern who is not like them.

The Word of God brings spiritual division between believers and unbelievers.

"Do you think I came to bring peace on earth? No, I tell you, but division." Luke 12:51

"For I came to SET A MAN AGAINST HIS FATHER, AND A DAUGHTER AGAINST HER MOTHER, AND A DAUGHTER-IN-LAW AGAINST HER MOTHER-IN-LAW; and A MAN'S ENEMIES WILL BE THE MEMBERS OF HIS HOUSEHOLD."
Matthew 10: 35-36

Now, less you think I don't understand your point of view. {Really, we should not have a point of view - either one of us. Our view should be God's view only, which will unite us.} Some use the argument that to operate in the natural world (versus the Kingdom), you have to know that your conversation and your actions must be neutral. I agree, but the problem comes when a believer encounters an unbeliever or an imposter or wannabee and does not recognize that fact. If they are not a true believer, they will start to feel uncomfortable – shut up to the faith. Eventually, they will let it be known that they feel uncomfortable talking about the Bible; that the believer needs to change. This is a litmus test of whether two can walk together.

"So then, you will know them by their fruits. "Not everyone who says to Me, 'Lord, Lord,' will enter the kingdom of heaven,…'" Matthew 7:20-21

The Bible tells believers many ways to recognize impostors or wannabees. *"We are from God, and whoever knows God listens to us; but whoever is not from God does not listen to us. This is how we recognize the Spirit of truth and the spirit of falsehood."* 1 John 4:6

We are not to marry persons outside the faith because there will be a constant battle between the believer and the unbeliever. Many unbelievers believe they are believers, but their behavior makes them out to be a liar (salt vs. salt substitute).

The entire reason God commanded the killing of men, women and children and cattle and destroying all possessions of the surrounding people was so the Israelite would not become infected with the disease of the people who did not worship the one true living God. *"Now go and attack the Amalekites and completely destroy everything they have. Do not spare them. Kill men and women, children and infants, oxen and sheep, camels and donkeys.'"* 1 Samuel 15:3

The union and love existing between a husband and wife should be like the union and love existing between Our LORD and His Church. The grace of the covenant vows a couple takes helps them to have such love. Even with both couples having saving grace, there will be pressures and weaknesses brought to bear on each party, on the family and on the marriage itself. "Weaknesses"—that is, their faults, bad dispositions, etc. will be strengthened by God and they will be enabled to bring up their children in the fear of the LORD. These are their most important duties, and parents who are saved receive grace to perform it, and woe unto them if they abuse that grace!

The Marriage Vows

The *wedding vows* are *covenant promises* made by the bride **and** groom to each other during a wedding ceremony, which we call Holy Matrimony. The two may choose to write their own wedding vows, rather than relying on standard wedding vow samples. Regardless, the vows consist of four basic parts: 1) affection (*love, comfort, keep*), 2) faithfulness (*forsaking all others*), 3 un- conditionality (*for richer or for poorer, in sickness and in health*), and 4) permanence (*as long as we both shall live, until death do us part*).

Affection (1 Corinthians 13). If I speak with human eloquence and angelic ecstasy but don't love, I'm nothing but the creaking of a rusty gate. If I speak God's Word with power, revealing all His mysteries and making everything plain as day, and if I have faith that says to a mountain, "Jump," and it jumps, but I don't love, I'm nothing. If I give everything I own to the poor and even go to the stake to be burned as a martyr, but I don't love, I've gotten nowhere. So, no matter what I say, what I believe, and what I do, I'm bankrupt without love.

Love never gives up. Love cares more for others than for self. Love doesn't want what it doesn't have. Love doesn't strut, Doesn't have a swelled head, Doesn't force itself on others, Isn't always "me first," Doesn't fly off the handle, Doesn't keep score of the sins of others, Doesn't revel when others grovel, Takes pleasure in the flowering of truth, Puts up with anything, Trusts God always, Always looks for the best, never looks back, But keeps going to the end.

Love never dies. Inspired speech will be over some day; praying in tongues will end; understanding will reach its limit. We know only a portion of the truth, and what we say about God is always incomplete. But when the Complete arrives, our incompletes will be canceled. When I was an infant at my mother's breast, I gurgled and cooed like any infant. When I grew up, I left those infant ways for good. But even as a human adult, we don't yet see things clearly. We're squinting in a fog, peering through a mist. But it won't be long before the weather clears and the sun shines bright! We'll see it all then, see it all as clearly as God sees us, knowing Him directly just as He knows us! But for right now, until that completeness, we have three things to do to lead us toward that consummation: Trust steadily in God, hope unswervingly, love extravagantly. And the best of the three is love.

Faithfulness (Mark 9:49-50). *"Everyone will be made cleaner and stronger with fire. Salt is good. But if salt loses its taste, how can it be made to taste like salt again? Have salt in yourselves and be at peace with each other."*

Faithfulness should be characteristic of God's people. Jesus used salt to illustrate three qualities that should be found in His people. 1) We should remember God's faithfulness just as salt used with a sacrifice recalled God's covenant with His people (Leviticus 2:13). 2) We should make a difference in the "flavor" of the world we live in: in our family, our children, our church and our jobs. We do not go looking for a blessing, but we go to be a blessing. We bring light into a world darkened by sin. We stay dressed in the Word by putting on the full armor of God so that we may be able to withstand. 3) We should counteract the moral decay in society, just as salt preserves food from decay. When we lose our desire to "salt" the earth with the love and message of God, we become useless to Him.

Un-conditionality (1 Peter 4:8). *"And above all things be earnest in your love among yourselves, for love covers a multitude of sins."*

Permanence [1 John 4:16]. *"And, as for us, we know the love which God has for us, and we confide in it. God is love, and he who continues to love continues in union with God, and God continues in union with him."*

And lastly, ask

What Makes You that Special Helper?

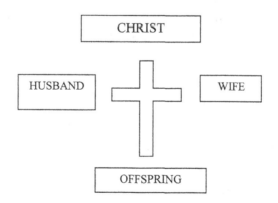

"Now about the question you asked in your letter. Yes, it is good to live a celibate life. But because there is so much sexual immorality, each man should have his own wife, and each woman should have her own husband" 1 Corinthians 7:1-2

Here is a scenario to ponder as you allow the Holy Spirit to lead you to recognize your lifetime companion. I want you to imagine that your ideal companion is somewhere in time and space praying to meet you. This individual feels ready to be a spouse and is asking God to bring to him someone that is trustworthy, kind, understanding, handles money well, works and is motivated and moving in their own ideas and gifts. He is asking for an individual who is humble, dependable and is devoted to showing their love in thoughtful ways; is respectful of their parents, even tempered and fair –minded; a real family oriented person, so to speak. From this prayer description, this individual is asking for a Godly person! Now, ask yourself, would God consider ME to fit the description for the individual who is praying? The bible says we should "Examine ourselves to see if we be in Christ?" 2 Corinthians 13:5

It's important that you understand that God is not going to take His child by the hand and present him to YOU (as He did Eve to Adam), if you are not seeking to live by His standards. I said "seeking" because no one is perfect, but we should be moving towards perfection and seeking to present ourselves as approved by God. All too often, we are too one-sided; judging other's weaknesses while there is a large plank in our own eye. As we move forward into the rest of this Hand Book, I want you to seriously examine yourself in each area to see if there are weaknesses that you may need to improve upon; so that you can become all that Christ would have you to be in the role of lifetime companion. After all, Christ is the head of a marriage relationship. Is Christ already navigating freely in your life? If so, are you ready to allow Him the same freedom to navigate in your marriage? Remember, He will be in charge of not just your partner, but you as well.

So what makes you different from any other woman he will certainly encounter now and in the future? Well, judge for yourself. Do you feel qualified to stand beside him? Has your mind and heart been captured by the things of God? Is Jesus your commander and chief – before and after marriage? Scripture tells us that Christians are aliens passing from this world into the next. Do you speak God's language? It is the language of love and encouragement. The good in you will encourage. You can't take back biting and hurtful words and actions after inflicting wounds. Do you see the lighter side of life? …preferring to cover and minimize mistakes. A Christian wife should be a positive influence on her spouse.

Are you a Proverbs 31 woman? Do you get up thinking about the good you can do for your family daily? Do you own a crockpot? Do you get up thinking about what you can put in it so that your family will be well fed at the end of the day? How about Spiritual food? Do you believe in home Bible study? Are you sharing grace for meals and prayer in the mornings and before bedtime? How are your emotions? Are they stable, or do you fly off the handle easily?

<u>Into the verse</u>: Because of their desire to serve Christ, some people in the Corinthian church thought they ought to divorce their pagan spouses and marry Christians. But Paul affirmed the marriage commitment. God's ideal is for marriages to stay together – even when one spouse is not a believer. The Christian spouse should try to win the other to Christ through their good Christian behavior (see fruit of the Spirit).

They should not bring pressure to change or make threats, demands or ultimatums. It would be easy to rationalize leaving; however, Paul makes a strong case for staying with the unbelieving spouse and being a positive influence on the marriage. Paul, like Jesus, believed that marriage is permanent. However, God would not encourage a spouse to remain to the detriment of her physical or mental health – or that of her children. (see *Mark 10:1-9*)

Aside from such detriments, if an unbelieving spouse is <u>encouraged</u> to look at what is unseen and not at what is seen (*2 Corinthians 4:18*), he should eventually look to Godly wisdom (and more to his spouse to help him figure things out). As he does this, he will begin to cultivate into his life the fruit of the spirit. The fruit of the Spirit (Galatians 5:22, 23; Ephesians 5:9; James 3:17, 18) are those gracious dispositions and habits which the Holy Spirit produces in those in whom He dwells and works. This may take some time; and a humble wife will see her husband's salvation as one of her missions in life.

If God's Spirit is drawing her spouse through her obedience, then she should see him turn more and more toward her (because He will recognize that God dwells within her through the outward fruit she is producing). It will throw him for a loop when she is not reacting the way of the world as he anticipates she will when he acts out.

"But the Holy Spirit produces this kind of fruit: love, joy, peace,
patience, kindness, goodness,
faithfulness, gentleness and self-control. There is no law against
these things." Galatians 5:22-23

Or if he is <u>discouraged</u> from an ungodly point of view (worldly reacting spouse), this means he is getting stress and anxiety from you – which is what he is getting from every other woman (including mother, sisters, aunts, etc.). By ungodly, I mean the wife is over lecturing, cursing/hollering as if she is his mother and being bossy, embarrassing him in front of others or talking about her man as "no good," to others, as a few examples. She feels justified because she is disappointed in him – or he started it first. A spiritually mature person will become an example to her spouse and seek out Godly advice when the need arises.

Many women do not understand that "every closed eye aint sleep." If her heart is not pure, she may be overheard saying negative things when she thinks he is not listening or is away. Many do not understand how the grapevine works, and may be surprised to learn that he knows exactly how she really feels because she is broadcasting it to persons who do not have her best interest or the best interest of the marriage at heart. If she is smiling in his face while talking against him, this adds insult to injury.

Withholding sex as punishment is very dangerous and forbidden in Scripture. Sex within marriage provides strength against temptations. Sexual temptations are difficult to withstand because they appeal to the normal and natural desires that God has given us. Marriage provides God's way to satisfy these natural sexual desires and to strengthen the partners against temptation. Married couples have the responsibility to care for each other; therefore, husbands and wives should not withhold themselves sexually from one another but should fulfill each other's needs and desires. Otherwise, adultery may produce venereal diseases, unwanted pregnancies [and accompanying child support issues], as well as the emotional roller coaster of emotional feelings of betrayal, anger, disillusionment, guilt and divorce.

Spiritually, our bodies belong to God when we become Christians because Jesus Christ bought us by paying the price to release us from sin (see 1 Corinthians 6:19-20). Physically our bodies belong to our spouses because God designed marriage so that, through the union of husband and wife, the two become one (*Genesis 2:24*). Paul stresses complete equality in sexual relationships. Neither male nor female shall seek to dominant or jump out of the marriage at signs of trouble.

A man, just like a woman, needs encouragement; he needs his wife to stand by his side and help him find his way. He does not need her to join the troop of naysayers who are tearing him down and making him feel unsure of himself. "*Be careful, or your hearts will be weighed down with dissipation, drunkenness and the anxieties of life, and that day will close on you unexpectedly like a trap.*" (Luke 21:34). Stress and/or lack of spiritual weapons cause him to make the choices he makes in the world—chooses addictions, lust, etc. If you are not for him, he will eventually turn away from you as one of those choices because you are "just like every other woman" he has known. No telling how many women have yelled foul play when they have actually driven or given their man away.

CHAPTER VIII

Does Intimacy Equal Infidelity?

Fidelity in Marriage

"But I tell you that anyone who looks at a woman lustfully has already committed adultery with her in his heart." Matthew 5:28

Fidelity is the quality of being faithful, loyal and steadfast to one's covenant promises. "Fidelity to one's marriage vows is absolutely essential for love, trust, and peace to thrive in the relationship. Adultery is unequivocally condemned by the Lord. "Husbands and wives who love each other will find that love and loyalty are reciprocated. This love will provide a nurturing atmosphere for the emotional and spiritual growth of children. Family life should be a time of happiness and joy that children can look back on with fond memories and associations."

Strict fidelity in marriage is essential in honoring the covenants we have made with our spouse and the Lord. There are precautions we can take to help us honor our marriage covenants. Remember,

- In the marriage ceremony, the spouses make covenant vows with each other and each individually and collectively with God.
- Fidelity in marriage is absolutely essential.
- Foreplay leading to sex begins sooner than you may think!

Case Study #1

Julia and Mark had a warm and affectionate relationship during the first year of their marriage. They were happy. Their first child was born early in the second year, and they both enjoyed being parents. Now, in the third year, they seldom hug or kiss or express any kind of physical affection for each other. Other than that their marriage is stable, they enjoy each other, and they work closely together to raise their child.

Julia, however, has developed a close friendship with their neighbor Gerald. There has been no physical intimacy between them except for a brief, one-time kiss. Because of the trials in their lives, Julia and Gerald find that they enjoy sitting together on the couch at Gerald's apartment and talking for an hour or two before Mark returns from work. Julia thoroughly enjoys being with Gerald and feels that she has complete control over her emotions. She is much happier in her own marriage since she has been receiving attention from Gerald. She is not concerned about breaking the law of chastity with Gerald because they have talked about it and each claims to love the Lord too much to do such a thing.

1. What is wrong with this relationship?
2. Is there any infidelity between Julia and Gerald? In what ways?
3. If Julia and Gerald's relationship goes no further physically, is it harmless?

Case Study #2

Malcolm likes the world of academics and hopes someday to teach at a university. He enjoys the rich interchange of ideas found in that setting. Since he finished his undergraduate program, his work and financial obligations have prevented him from seeking an advanced degree. He is disappointed that his wife Kendra, with whom he shared so much during their courtship, no longer enjoys reading and talking about world issues. The children and house take up much of her time. By sharing his books and ideas with his friends at work and being involved in a weekly book club, Malcolm has been able to fill his needs. Sheila, a young woman from work, joined the club after hearing about it from Malcolm. Malcolm especially enjoys the insights that Sheila contributes.

4. Is there infidelity between Malcolm and Sheila in this arrangement?
5. What are the potential dangers?
6. What can Malcolm do to build a better relationship with his wife?

Case Study #3

After they married, David was surprised to discover that his new wife Annah liked to stay at home most of the time. David has always loved sports and the outdoors. Annah, though, loves keeping house and taking care of David and their baby. David plays for a local sports team, and sometimes Annah is unhappy with the number of evenings it keeps him away. Several weekends a month he goes fishing. Once he even saved his money for months to buy Annah a fishing pole and waders and tried to teach her to fish. Annah tried to show interest but never really enjoyed it. David wishes Annah were more like Lisa, a young woman at work who loves to play and talk sports. Lisa attends many of his sporting events.

7. What are the danger signals in this marriage?
8. What are possible solutions to the problem?

Case Study #4

Robert, a married member of the Church with two young daughters, enjoys surfing the Internet late in the evening when everyone is asleep. He recently happened on a site with pornographic materials. Although it was offensive at first glance, he found himself drawn into it. For the next several evenings, after everyone was asleep, he returned to that site and additional sites with similar material.

One night his wife, Barbara, came into the room and caught him looking at pornography. She was devastated and became angry. She insisted on an appointment with the bishop and threatened to divorce Robert. Robert knows what he was doing was wrong but feels that Barbara is overreacting.

9. Where do you think Robert erred?

10. Why is Robert's behavior serious?

11. What can Robert do to rebuild his wife's confidence in him and strengthen their marriage?

12. At what point would you recommend Robert seek personal counseling?

13. What are ways that pornography can destroy a marriage?

I pause to remind the bride and groom that not just one but both make promises before God and man. Therefore, each is held equally responsible for the keeping of these vows. If one breaks a vow, the other is not then free to break their vows. "If he can cheat on me, I can do it to."

However, we cannot overlook that an injured spouse has been given a choice to divorce if adultery is involved (Matthew 5:31–32). But, this author advocates that you look for ways to restore a marriage rather than leave it. Jesus said that divorce is not permissible except for unfaithfulness. This does not mean that divorce should automatically occur when a spouse commits adultery. The word translated "unfaithful" implies a sexually immoral lifestyle, not a confessed and repented act of adultery.

Those who discover that their partner has been unfaithful should first make every effort to forgive, reconcile, and restore their relationship. We are always to look for reasons to restore the marriage relationship rather than for excuses to leave it. Your final choices and decisions should be carefully weighed and discussed with God and also with worthy mentors.

CHAPTER IX

Relationship Dynamics: Distinguishing Abuse from True Love

Law of Attraction

In the world of Quantum Physics - thoughts (positive or negative) attract their equivalent or vibrational match. Think good thoughts attract good things. Think bad, negative or needy thoughts and you'll attract bad, negative and needy situations into your life. In short, to attract your ideal mate, you must possess all the qualities you desire in that individual. Because, whatever you focus on with intensity and your <u>emotions</u> will set the Universe in motion to bring that into your life. No wonder Scripture tells us "Fix your thoughts on what is true, and honorable, and right, and pure, and lovely, and admirable. Think about things that are excellent and worthy of praise." (Philippians 4:8) Emotion is a key here, and your emotions come from your thought life. Most of us send out far stronger emotional signals about the things we don't want than those we do want. And that's normal. It's how you and I are wired and it takes very deliberate thinking to overcome our emotional hard-wiring.

And that's normal. It's how you and I are wired and it takes very deliberate thinking to overcome our emotional hard-wiring.

I believe God has someone special for everyone. It will be your job to recognize your match with a godly fear. James 1:5 says *"If anyone lacks wisdom, you should ask God, who gives generously to all without finding fault, and it will be given to you."*

Many marriages prove unhappy because they are entered into *hastily* and without *worthy motives*. **"Hastily,"** meaning without knowing the person well or considering their character or dispositions; without trying to discover whether they are sober, industrious, virtuous, and the like; whether they are saved and practice their religion, or whether, on the contrary, they are given to vices forbidden by good morals, and totally forgetful of their religious duties.

In a word, those wishing to marry should look for enduring qualities in their lifelong companions, and not for characteristics that please the fancy for the time being. The couple should, besides, truly love each other. The persons should be nearly equals in age, education, social standing, etc., for it helps greatly to secure harmony between families and unity of thought and action between themselves.

"Worthy motives," meaning the motives are worthy when persons marry to fulfill the end for which God instituted marriage. It would, for example, be a destructive motive to marry solely for looks, money, property, or other advantages, without any regard for the holiness and end of the Covenant you are entering into. There are many motives that may present themselves to the minds of persons wishing to marry, and you will know whether they are worthy or unworthy, good or bad, if by serious consideration you soberly weigh them well and value these motives by their desire to please God and lead a good life.

To this endeavor, every person's motive in getting married or in entering into any new state of life should be that they may be better able to serve God in that state than in the previous state.

The following areas are not meant to be exhaustive but to give you a flavor of how you should be thinking and what types of dynamics you should be alert to as you are interact with a love interest.

This door swings both ways, so be aware of what you are bringing into a relationship; whether you are at a stage in your life that you are ready and willing to fulfill the dreams and imaginations of a godly companion. After all, a balanced relationship is what you are looking for, isn't it? And may the Lord bless you and keep you in every endeavor.

Reflection #1: Accountability

The way of a fool is right in his own eyes, but he that listens to counsel is wise. Proverbs 12:15

Purpose: The one you wish to marry should be someone who will not ignore the counsel of worthy mentors. He should be someone who surrounds himself with people of excellence (persons who are mentally healthy and well-adjusted). He should strive to be like those who are the children and people of God.

Definition. Worthy mentors may be described as individuals who possess spiritual wisdom, walk with God and whose feet do not sit in the counsel of the ungodly nor stand in the way of sinners or sit in the seat of mockers.) But their delight is in the Law of the Lord. (Psalm 1)

LORD, I know that people's lives are not their own; it is not for them to direct their steps. Jeremiah 10:23

You've got to ask God for His wisdom because everybody talking about Heaven ain't going there. You must judge the company you keep. There is a dark side that people can choose to keep hidden. Whoever you hang out with will influence your thoughts and actions. If you're not the stronger, you'll be overruled by someone else's moral values and standards. You can easily fall back into the lifestyle God brought you out of, if you do not continue to seek His presence in your life.

Defining moments: If you feel your love one ignores worthy counsel from qualified mentors in his life, you will also suffer the consequences. Who are his heros? Everyone strives to become like those they admire. You seek to adapt the habits and convictions of those you envy. Who is his dominant mentor? At whose feet does he sit consistently? A mentor is a Prophecy or a Protégé. If they rebel against the council of their pastor, they are living undisciplined, uncovered and unadvised. Tragedy is scheduled. It's just a matter of time.

Study the kind of people that he surrounds himself with. If you feel people of excellence do not surround him, this may be an indication he is not motivated to excellence. If these people appear to be strange bedfellows to you, this is a clue to his lifestyle. It is also a clue to your future with him and the people he will want you to associate with. Healthy well-adjusted people should be able to inspire confidence in his abilities while seeming modest and likable.

You will not do well in forming a permanent relationship with an individual who has not impressed qualified mentors. It's best to inquire with family members, employers, friends—anyone who can help you have a more well-rounded opinion about this individual. Watch guarded speech from those who may not want to say anything unkind or cause trouble in the relationship. Be aware that something deeper is going on, if there is an effort to guard feedback to questions you may ask about your love interest.

Beware if your love one refuses to sit consistently under the mentorship of spiritual leadership. Spiritual growth will not occur without worthy mentors or uncommon pain. Unwillingness to sit under the mentorship of proven mentors (persons who have gone through uncommon pain and have yielded to God's unchanging hand), is a devastating revelation of potential failure in the relationship.

> *"Her husband is respected at the city gate, where he takes his seat*
> *among the elders of the land."* (Proverbs 31;23)

If you do not admire and respect the mentors at whose feet your love one sits, he will feel threatened by you. His mentors are either feeding strength or a weakness in him. Either one is an extension of his perceived self. If you oppose his mentor, he will feel you are opposing him and his right to make his own choices and decisions. A relationship with him will be made impossible.

Remember that worthy mentors can help advise your love one against temptation if he becomes attracted to any vice. If he is in rebellion and leading a bad life, the saved companion will have no means of reaching the root of the evil, no hope that he may take the advice of worthy mentors, or seek godly counseling or do any of those things that could affect a change in their heart and life.

Reflection #2: Beauty, Inner

"Charm is deceitful, and beauty is vain, but a woman who fears the LORD is to be praised."
Proverbs 31:30

Purpose: An ideal companion should be very interested in attending to your contentment and happiness. He must have a relationship with God because God is the only one that can cause faithfulness in marriage – looks will not, sex will not and neither will kindness.

Attractiveness cannot guarantee faithfulness. The fear of God keeps us faithful. It is sad to read magazine articles that teach the art of deception, manipulation, illusion, and intimidation to capture and/or keep another. A woman should not believe that her looks can hold a man because there are plenty of good looking women around. Beauty will not. How foolish if you believe you can keep your appearance so attractive, that the one you wish to marry will not look at another. Your attractiveness does not make another person ugly!

"But the Lord said to Samuel, "Do not consider his appearance or his height,
for I have rejected him." The LORD does not look at the things people look at.
People look at the outward appearance, but the LORD
looks at the heart." 1 Samuel 16:7

Defining moments: Physical appearance is important to us and we spend time and money improving it, but real beauty is inside. How much effort do we put into developing our inner beauty? Patience, kindness and joy are the beauty treatments that help us become truly lovely – on the inside. The most enhancing feature on the outside is a smile.

Real beauty affects others positively. A changed life speaks loudly and clearly, and it is often the most effective way to influence a spouse or family member. Peter instructs Christian wives to develop inner beauty rather than being overly concerned about their outer appearance (1Peter 3:3-4). Their husbands will be won over by their love rather than by their looks. We should live our Christian faith quietly and consistently in our homes, and our family will see Christ in us.

We should not be obsessed by fashion, but neither should we be so unconcerned that we do not bother to care for ourselves. Hygiene, neatness and grooming are important. But even more important is a person's attitude and spirit. True beauty begins inside and is reflected on the outside.

Real beauty is not self-centered. In first Timothy chapter two verses one through ten, apparently some Christian women were trying to gain respect by looking beautiful rather than by becoming Christ-like in character. Some may have thought that they could win unbelieving husbands to Christ through their appearance (pay close attention to Peters' counsel in chapter three verses one through six). It is not unscriptural for a woman to want to be attractive. Beauty, however, begins inside of a person. A gentle, modest, loving character gives a light to the face that cannot be duplicated by the best cosmetics and jewelry in the world. A carefully groomed and well-decorated exterior is artificial and cold unless inner beauty is present.

If your love one is attracted to you only for your physical abilities and looks, this individual is a surface person. As you age, your lifetime companion will wander to greener pastures.

Reflection #3: Character Study

And now, my daughter, don't be afraid. I will do for you all you ask.
All the people of my town know that you are a woman of noble character. Ruth 3:11

Purpose: Positive character traits in an ideal companion should include a mate who can empathize and comfort; and shows pain or remorse concerning past mistakes and sins; one who has exited previous relationships without conflict, and someone who keeps his promises.

Definition: Character may be described as the attributes that make a person who they are. I've heard it said that the real measure of a person's character is what they do if they knew they would never be found out. I tend to agree. Character traits are the distinguishing marks that show an individual to be a person of high or low moral values. Ideally, what is said, thought and done should line up with what a person says they believe. For instance, a person who says they are a man of God should not lie or steal because the Bible says these things are wrong. A true indication of who a person is comes through in what they do, not in what they say, because thoughts come before actions.

Defining moments. Don't judge a love interest by his looks, a fancy job description or his car. These thing, while they meet needs, do not say much about who he is inside. You should think about it very carefully if he laughs at things that ordinarily should cause sadness. He is showing that he is unable to empathize, or put himself in the shoes of others.

When tragedy strikes others, if he makes comments such as "that's good enough for them?" Or "God is not mocked" without knowing the details, you should wonder about his true feelings towards you if you should ever fail in a certain area (suffer a loss of employment, identity theft, sickness, etc.). How will he respond?

*"For we hear of some who walk among you in rebellion, who don't
work at all but are busybodies." 2 Thessalonians 3:11*

If your love interest shows little pain or remorse concerning past mistakes and sins, he is not truly repentant or hurt in any way. Repentant people are not ignorant of the personal choices and deeds that have led them to their present circumstances. Repentant people do not blame other people for their choices and decisions. The memories of their mistakes should produce sorrow and heartache, not bitter accusations. Be careful of this kind of individual. Being involved with someone is not supposed to get you raped and/or killed.

When regret is not expressed, the offense usually occurs again. Some people never repent for past mistakes. Why? They have not truly tasted the painful consequences of their own rebellion. He sees his present situation more as a setback and temporary. This means he does not possess a true fear of God. He believes he is beyond judgment. It is futile to pursue a relationship with someone who does not possess an obvious fear of God. Lack of fear of God means lack of fear period. Uncorrected conduct becomes repeated conduct.

*"A good man brings good things out of the good stored up in his heart,
and an evil man brings evil things out of the evil stored up in his heart.
For the mouth speaks what the heart is full of." Luke 6:45*

<u>Men behind Bars</u>. Extreme caution is advised if you are reading letters/listening to a love interest that is behind bars. A person's true character cannot be observed in such a structured setting. His free will and ability to make choices has been taken away from him. You can only take their word that he has or will change. Observations after release to observe whether he returns to his old patterns of coping and behaving are highly recommended. The author recommends 12 months.

If there are signs that your love interest has not exited previous relationships peacefully, this person suffers from credibility gaps. Watch comments such as, "I wasn't given a say in the matter," or "I really didn't want to, but …" Many people thrive on strife, which means they enjoy it! They will destroy anything they cannot own or control. Peace bores them. Silence nauseates them and makes those who practice it in their presence appear foolish and weak (see 1 Cor. 2:14). They will speak any words necessary to push the boundary lines and limitations around them. Many of these persons were raised in strife filled and violent homes and feel that the only way the other can show their love is by practicing actions that provoke conflict and violence against them - the same way they perceive it was portrayed in their childhood home. It will be impossible to enjoy a peaceful relationship with this individual because it is not what they perceive as "normal."

"Let your yes be yes and your no, no. Whatever is more than this is of the evil one."
Matthew 5:37

If your love one breaks promises to you or to others easily and voluntarily, he is aware of the things that he falls short of. Perhaps, he has the best of intentions at the time the promise is made. If you or others are putting pressure on him for which he later renege on, then you are setting yourselves up for failure each time. He may have good intentions, or may be lying just to get the pressure off at the time. God has given each free will. It is useless to try to change someone or attempt to force someone to do something before they are ready.

If your love interest corrects you without reminding you that he loves you, he has no regard for keeping your heart open through forgiveness and mercy. This individual has no regard for your feelings if he continues to reason with you or attempts to give you an explanation when you are upset or angry. He may even feel manipulation is easier when you are upset. One powerful form of manipulation is flattery or sugary words intended to build you up for a big let-down. Under no circumstances should you engage in any conversation where flattery is used to make you change your mind.

Think twice if your love one uses foul language when he is upset because this shows disrespect, a desire to shock and control, and/or a lack of education which manifests in being unable or unwilling to find more creative ways of expressing themselves, such as "Oh shucks!" "Gee whiz." Or "That lights a match under my toe!"

If your love one continuously gives you advice that is contrary to the Word of God, he is causing you to have to choose whom you will serve. The Word of God is Truth. It will withstand any test. The Word destroys wrong desires within you; unleashes your faith and produces hope. The Word purifies your mind. The Word is the master key to all success on earth. Your reaction to the Word of God determines God's reaction to you and to your own children.

"My people are being destroyed because they don't know me. Since you priests
refuse to know me, I refuse to recognize you as my priests. Since you have
forgotten the laws of your God, I will forget to bless your children." (Hosea 4:6)

We know that nothing has so bad an influence upon people as bad company. In the case of a saved companion, she may resist his evil influence for a time, but will, if not very steadfast in faith yield to it; and, tired of numerous disputes in defense of her religious rights, will become more and more indifferent, gradually giving up the practice of worship, and probably terminating with complete loss of faith or apostasy from the church, just to please her spouse. This is true because there is always the more likelihood that the bad will pervert the good, rather than the good converting the bad. God will become an enemy with continued efforts to defy His Word. It would be tragic to bond with someone God may ultimately destroy. For this person may take you and your children right along with him.

Reflection #4: Children

Children are a heritage from the LORD, offspring a reward from him. Proverbs 127:3

Purpose. An ideal companion will understand that children are a gift from God. Parents brought their children into the world so they do owe them something. But what and how much is the most challenging balancing act for parents. Besides the basic necessities of life (food, clothing and shelter), parents owe their children love, respect, discipline, self-discipline, a sense of being valued, education, and patience. Parents also owe their children the opportunity to develop their Spiritual gifts and skills which are necessary to become successful adults. To prevent her children's suffering as well as her self, a single mother should make every effort to check out a new love interest – from making the courtship process a long one in order to check out his character/patterns of behavior, his thoughts on critical issues and his tolerance levels; to checking feedback from family members, friends, his preacher, – even to hiring a private investigator, if necessary, to check out his background. Does he work and have an enduring job history? Is he willing to support step kids?

Defining moments. Children shouldn't have to suffer from their mother's bad decisions and choices. If so, they may get mixed up in the welfare and foster care systems and may suffer harm that parents cannot begin to fathom.

Because of our modern world thinking and the economy, please do not take it for granted that your love one is interested in either raising your children or having children with you. Being ready to take on all the responsibilities of raising a family is a huge decision, and taking on a ready-made one brings on additional burdens that some men will feel ill equipped to handle. Some men that are interested in you may feel anywhere from ambivalent to downright hostile towards your children.

Also, the extent that this individual feels his involvement should be in raising any children – yours or his and yours together- is extremely important. Your love interest may have grown up in a household where only one companion was responsible for the raising and disciplining of children; or children were sent off to boarding school or raised by grandparents. Forming enduring bonds is the last thing on his mind. If your children are unable to get close, neither will you. Many have overlooked these important issues and lived to regret it.

As a single mom, not only do you have to be concerned about whether you are making the right decision for yourself, but you come as a package deal that cannot be separated. Child molesters and pedophiles look as ordinary as the next person, but they are very real. According to police reports, they like hanging around single, vulnerable women who could use some help with their kids. Most prey on those closest to them, their own or their stepchildren. Mother, you must be vigilant. Never let a new love interest meet your kids – male or female – until you are absolutely sure he is a mature and right thinking man. Make it clear to him how you are a mother first and stand your ground. Many mothers have chosen to wait until her kids are in college before marrying.

If you are a single mom, your male children need a male mentor to help them grow beyond the nurturing stage into spiritual maturity.

> *"And Satan himself is transformed into an angel of light. It is no great thing*
> *for his servants also to disguise themselves as servants of righteousness.*
> *Their end will be in accordance with their actions."* (2 Corinthians 11:14-15)

At any rate, stay close to your kids so they will defy someone who tells them "Don't tell Mama." Know your kids well enough to sense when they are acting different. Even though no one would question that you are a good mother, you can be fooled. Your love interest may act wonderful with the kids in your presence, but what is he like when you are not around? Ask your kids about him. God gave them feelings and rights. In the case of even very young children, do they cry or act afraid when they hear he's coming over? Don't just assume they dislike him because he is someone new in your life. Pay attention to covert behavior.

Take a pass on living together without marriage. Cohabitation means "I don't want to be committed." Or "I will be here as long as things are going good." But if you are already living together, pay attention to what may be going on right under your nose. Is your love interest always trying to spend time with your children – without you around? Does he want your son to spend the night over at his place? Have you ever caught him hanging around your daughter's room at night? Has he ever "accidentally" barged in on her while she is taking a bath? Does he want to display bedroom behavior or talk dirty in front of your kids? Does he want to show dirty movies during family time? If so, you have a freak on your hands.

Keep eyes and ears open. Ask him how he feels about children in general. Does he want kids of his own? If you really feel that you are not going to have any more babies and your love interest wants his own flesh and blood offspring, he may come to resent yours. Something worse, he may "accidentally" father a child with another woman.

Does he already have children from a previous relationship? If so, how will they feel about you and your children?

Does he know anything about children? Has he ever dealt with a sick or fussy child? How are his tolerance and compassion levels? Will he become abusive under stress?

In the case of children (adults or otherwise, on either side, how the love interest treats their own children should be looked at very carefully – do they come before you? Also, is there an attempt to divide you from the love and affection of your own children or extended family? This will not get better over time, but spells disaster just waiting to happen.

Be sure you agree on how children should be disciplined before you bring a love interest into your household. Disciplining your kids is not only your job, but your ideas about what constitutes discipline may be wildly different.

Parents are the first authority in a child's life. Friendship often clashes with authority, especially in young children. But a balance must be maintained. Give your children the gift of being allowed to express themselves. This will frustrate their need to resort to physical violence and serve them well throughout life as a problem-solving tool.

> *"Fathers do not exasperate your children; instead, bring them up in*
> *the fear of the LORD."* (Ephesians 6:4)

If parents provoke their children to disobedience; they will become disobedient to authority (teachers, principals, police, etc.) If your child becomes disobedient to authority, without intervention they will become disobedient to the ultimate authority, which is their Maker God. If they become disobedient to God, they will become His enemy which He will ultimately have to destroy.

Children should be taught that their parents have received special grace from God to advise, direct, and warn them of sin; and if they refuse to obey their parents or despise their direction, they are despising God's grace. Remember that nothing teaches as well as experience.

Children are taught more by the behavior of the adults in their life than the lectures they receive. If your love one is disobedient and arrogant, you have a fifty-fifty chance that the children will be disobedient and arrogant as well. Children should be taught that their parents have experience. They have been children as they are; they have been young persons as they are; they have received advice from their parents and teachers as they are now receiving. If parents are bad (addicted, living undisciplined, etc.), it is because they have not heeded the advice given them. If they are good, it is because they have heeded and followed wise counsel.

> *"The earth is the LORD's, and the fullness thereof; the world, and*
> *they that dwell therein."* Psalm 24:1

Your children, like you, belong to God. You are their caretaker; they are not your property. God wants you to show them the way to Him by loving them the way He does. He also wants you to help them find their gifts within and guide them to His plan for their life. Balance here is also important. Ask yourself "Are my expectations for my children realistic considering their individual strengths and weaknesses?" "Do my children have the God-given talent to fulfill my expectations?" "Do I want what's best for my children, or do I want what's best for me?"

Remember, your children will grow up, and should leave the nest one day, but a companion should be there to stay. Do not make decisions concerning your children that make them want to remain permanently with you.

Children learn best from watching; not from lecturing. How you treat your spouse; and more importantly your own parents will determine how your children learn to treat you when they are adults.

Criticizing your children's father to them/or where they can hear, may set them up for failure in the long run; 50% of who they are is you and the other 50% of them is their father. When you criticize that father, are you criticizing that 50% of the child? If you ignore this and criticize anyway, you set up dissonance (discord; an instance of disagreement with what we hear and what we see with our own eyes) in the child that will begin to manifest in role confusion, lack of motivation, anger, etc. They may not feel that they can talk back to you, but inside they are exploding with pent up emotions.

Train up a child in the way he should go: and when he is old, he will not depart from it. Proverbs 22:6

Parents have an obligation to introduce their children to the world of work. When it comes to rearing children, a parent must be able to envision a child as an adult. See their end from the beginning. Don't be surprised, if you do not take the time to show your child how money is made and why when they are young, when they grow up to be lazy unmotivated couch potatoes.

A word concerning **YOU as your parent's child**: Parents will believe it an injustice to them if their son or daughter marries into families that may have been disgraced, or that may bring disgrace upon them.

On the other hand, however, parents can be unreasonable in this matter: they may be proud or vain, and want to suit themselves rather than their children. Sometimes, too, they force marriage upon their children, or forbid it for purely worldly or selfish motives. In such cases, and indeed in all cases, the best one to consult and ask advice from is your pastor or a worthy mentor. He or she has only your spiritual interests at heart, and will set aside all worldly motives. If your parents are unreasonable, a godly counselor will be a just judge in the matter, and tell you how to decide and behave.

Reflection #5: Communications

Do not let any unwholesome talk come out of your mouths,
but only what is helpful for building others up according to their needs,
that it may benefit those who listen. Ephesians 4:29

<u>Purpose:</u> Positive communication traits in an ideal companion should include someone whose conversation energizes you to want to do your best. An ideal companion should be someone who listens and tries to understand your point of view, does not give you advice contrary to the Word of God, and someone who values your point of view and seeks out your advice. Your love interest should long to pleasure you. He should seek every opportunity to communicate through touching, gift giving, and spending time with you. Do not over-compensate in these areas. It's not what goes in, but what comes out that defiles.

Definition. Communication is defined as a process by which information is exchanged between individuals through a common system of symbols, signs, or behavior. It can also be defined as the means by which you engage a person, not necessarily orally but through body language and actions. How you engage a person should manifest the love of God within you. However, in order to ensure that communication is effective, the parties involved have to make sure that information is conveyed and received in the way in which it is intended. In order to make this happen, we must develop the capacity to set boundaries. We must be concerned with the impact our conversation is having on the person we are communicating with. Consider the following scenarios very seriously before taking that major step towards matrimony.

"Do not be tricked by false words; evil company does damage to good behavior."
(1 Corinthians 15:33)

Defining moments. Something has gone out of the relationship if your love interest no longer understands or pleasures you when you try to have a conversation. Somehow your feelings of frustration show that you have come down off of cloud 9 long enough to realize something is wrong.

Beware of such statements such as "I'll be glad when we get married so I can tell you what I really think." Your intended lifetime companion is apparently putting on a façade for now – just waiting until after marriage to show you their true selves.

Something is wrong if conversation with him has become burdensome, and leaves you frazzled and exhausted. It's not just what is being said; it's who is doing the talking. Right people should energize you. Wrong people will exhaust you, while true love will make you feel that you can do anything you put your mind to!

Think about it seriously if he raises his voice when he gets upset, he is showing a lack of self-control which may eventually lead to physical violence, especially if he advance towards you and/or clenches his teeth or balls up his fists while speaking.

If your love one makes sarcastic remarks about you (For instance, "You don't have sense enough to come out of the rain," or "You need to lose weight,' or "You got issues," etc.), he no longer celebrates your presence in his life and has one foot out of the door already.

One woman explained that God gave her a vision that her potential mate was going to be in a car accident. She tried to explain this to him, but he began cursing and said he didn't want to hear that! Less than 30 minutes later, he was in an accident just as she had seen it in her vision. As he tells it later, his whole life flashed before his eyes. He was apologetic and brought home flowers and candy that evening.

Your opinion is not important and neither are you, if he is unwilling to follow your personal advice or counsel. This individual needs to understand and recognize that a godly lifetime companion is the Prophetess in his bosom; you should be wells of wisdom for each other. Without this understanding, respect is absent.

Reflection #6: Conduct

The way of the guilty is devious, but the conduct of the innocent is upright.
Proverbs 21:8

Purpose: An ideal companion should be someone who is consistent in action and speech. He should be someone who does not enjoy the environment of rebels, smoke filled, curse saturated atmospheres, but one who is serious about the Word of God and the consequences of sin. He should be someone who is able to keep confidences and is discrete. It should also be someone who respects and treats you like a lady whose heart is fragile and can be broken.

Definition. Conduct may be described as a personal way of behaving or being in relationship with another. It may also be described as the set of interpersonal skills used to maintain relationships. How a person behaves may be said to be a truer indication of who he is rather than what he says. Reliability and consistency in a companion are the keys before making a final decision towards anything permanent.

"And Satan himself is transformed into an angel of light. It is no great thing for his servants also to disguise themselves as servants of righteousness. Their end will be in accordance with their actions." (2 Corinthians 11:14–15)

Defining moments. If your love one shows inconsistency in action and speech, he has something to hide. He either does not remember prior actions and speech or was not sincere (lying) at the time. For instance, if he does not mind stealing the iron from a hotel room while reminding you that you should not steal, something is wrong with his thinking.

If he speaks carelessly without considering the implications of what is being said, he is not thinking on a deeper level. In other words, he speaks without thinking. He may be a chauvinist or a feminist who believes it makes him appear stronger to shoot off at the mouth, especially about private things that should be kept between the two of you. "Let the chips fall where they may" or "If the shoe fits, wear it," is his motto.

When you are truly in love, that's all you want to talk about. If you are not excited about introducing your loved one to those you care about, either you are ashamed of your friends, or you are ashamed of him.

If he enjoys the atmosphere of rebels, he is not offended by sin. Anything that grieves God should grieve us. A person can be quite appealing, classy, elegant, knowledgeable, attractive, and a brilliant conversationalist. But, if he enjoys the company of others who are obvious sinners, or defend their rights to be different, or with whomever they please, then he has not settled these same issues within themselves.

> *"And withal they learn to be idle, wandering about from house to house; and not only*
> *idle, but tattlers also and busybodies, speaking things which they ought not."*
> (1Timothy 5:13)

If your love one finds breaking the law humorous and exciting, there is no sense of remorse in him. When you hear someone bragging about the "time when" they committed a crime or got over in a previous relationship, you should recognize that you are in the presence of someone who despises restraint, sneers at the law and wants the world to know about it.

If he becomes excited in the atmosphere of unbelievers, (able to relax, smile and talk easily), this means the atmosphere of the ungodly excites his flesh and causes him to feed on such things as nude bars, X-rated movies, and smoke-filled cuss-saturated, filthy joking, beer-drinking crowds?

If your favorite atmosphere is the house of God, with hands uplifted, loving, praising and worshipping the One who created you, you have no future with someone who insists of fueling their passion in the atmosphere of the ungodly. This is whom he identifies with. He will not mix with, or be able to fellowship within the house of God for very long.

> *"A good man shows favor; and lends to those in need; He will guide his affairs*
> *with discretion."* (Psalms 112:5)

If your love one does not keep confidential matters, you should fear he may have a problem keeping personal, confidential matters concerning your relationship. Keeping confidences speaks volumes about character. Observing discretion in your love one speaks volumes about his character. Observing discretion in the one who decides to keep quiet about hurtful or personal information involving others can carry over to other favorable conclusions about his credibility in times of conflict or stress.

"And you are of your father the devil... When he speaks a lie, he speaks of his own:
for he is a liar, and the Father knows it." (John 8:44)

If he lies or exaggerates, he loses credibility. If you have observed his willingness to lie, regardless of the reason, you should wonder whether he will always tell you the truth in a tight spot. For instance, I once knew a man who stole his wife's credit cards and ran them up to get money. Even though she was hurt, she listened to his explanation and took him back. Although she understood on a head level that this man took money that should have been used to maintain the household, her heart refused to believe that the real reason was that he was addicted and would continue to steal, lie and do whatever he needed to do to maintain the habit. This woman ended up losing her home and the lifestyle to which she was accustomed before she accepted the truth and left him.

Reflection #7: Cruelty/Anger

"Deliver me not over unto the will of mine adversaries:
For false witnesses are risen up against me,
And such as breathe cruelty." (Psalms 27:12)

Purpose: An ideal companion should be someone who has his emotions under control; who is not easily angered or allows molehills to become mountains. Your intended should be someone that respects you as a person, does not tease or joke at your expense, and treasures you as a created human being with gifts and values.

Definition. Cruelty can be described as indifference to suffering, and even positive pleasure in inflicting it. Anger may be described as feelings buried alive. Our wrong reactions to painful situations are just the symptoms of a deeper problem that we may, over time, forget. But the response is still there.

Defining moments. You should think twice if he calls you unkind names when he becomes angry. This is a sign of disrespect and a clue to how He has learned to respond to the opposite sex. It is also a lack of social skills which will manifest in inflexibility in the use of language skills and an unwillingness to change. It doesn't matter how much schooling (higher education or school of hard knocks) he's acquired; has he learned what needed to be learned? The Bible calls it *"always learning but never able to come to the knowledge of the truth."* (2 Timothy 3:7)

Think twice if your love interest teases you excessively alone and/or in front of others. If he does, he is using this as a disguised form of communicating his true feelings about something that might otherwise be confrontational and unpleasant. In other words, there is something he wants to tell you, but only feels safe saying it in front of others and in the form of "just joking." Teasing and joking at your expense are forms of cruelty. Cruelty is the opposite of love.

> *"The trouble he causes shall return to his own head. His violence shall come down on his own head."* (Psalm 7:16)

If your love one ever uses brute force (shoving, pushing or hitting, he does not value your physical well-being; and will eventually cause irreparable damage or death. It is best to find a safe way out immediately. Even if this person just likes to horseplay or touches you in degrading ways, this is a sign of disrespect and cruelty, especially if it continues after you've asked him to stop. This type of behavior may eventually lead to other forms of more serious physical cruelty, such as slapping, hitting and pinching; which he will blame on you because you accidentally scratched him while trying to ward off his physical advances during "horseplay."

Pick up the phone and call the police or your local department of social services and they will direct you or take you to a shelter or other sources of help. Please use discretion about whom you tell your plans to; and do not tell your companion what you are planning to do because he will try to stop you. Remember

> *"The righteous cry and the LORD hears and delivers them out of all their troubles. The LORD is close to the brokenhearted and saves those who are crushed in spirit."* (Psalms 34:17-18)

If your love interest takes you for granted, he does not appreciate your contributions to the relationship. He is the most important one in the relationship and is overly secure in believing you will always be there, no matter what. You can expect to spend lots of time alone or in the company of his companions.

If he continuously tells you how to do things you are already quite capable of doing on your own, he does not believe you have skills and abilities worth paying attention to.

Your relationship is temporary if he continuously nags you to improve in certain areas. This person is not satisfied with the way you already are. He may stay because he "sees" great potential, or stay for other things like what you have to offer in the forms of money, security, etc. But be sure to understand that these things may keep him in place – for a while, but he will never accept you as you are. Just don't forget that these things can be found in others besides you. It's just a matter of time.

You should think twice if he bosses you around as if you are a subordinate in the military. You are not valued as a thinking, breathing person. Neither is your opinion. Love ones don't live with members of the military; they only tolerate them because of a shared interest. He may be living out a macho fantasy that will become embarrassing in front of others.

If he continuously ignores your presence (moves and acts as though you are not around), he does not value your presence; he is simply tolerating you until better comes along.

If your love interest treats you harshly by yelling or advancing towards you in a menacing way when disapproving or angry with you, he is failing to show empathy or compassion for you as a fallible human being. He will continuously hold you responsible for things he, as a fallible human being, is unable to live up to in himself. At any rate, the advancing should be taken seriously because it is a sign of a person being one step away from using violence—if you say or do the wrong thing.

If this individual shows impatience, which may come across as rudeness, this shows disrespect, a desire to control, and/or a lack of humility. This means he has not yielded his rights to the Lord Jesus Christ already. He is unable to wait for Christ to return his expectations to him in His own timing, and as undeserved blessings. He wants everything to be perfect right now.

Every companion has certain expectations, not only in their own life and ministry, but also of others. In not attempting to "play God' in their own life or in the lives of others, a humble person will yield to the Lord even some very good and appropriate goals. A companion must know that God will use a delay of fulfillment to accomplish what He desires in order to prevent self-blame or blaming of others.

A companion must also realize that the Lord will motivate their mate to delay gratification by using the demands of their companion or other people. A companion must know it is really to the LORD that they are yielding their rights to and not necessarily to other people.

Your feelings are not important if your love interest says "no" without feeling that he needs to give you a reason; and therefore, you are not important.

If your love interest cuts down things you are doing or planning (with or without giving an explanation), or cuts down someone you spend time with, he has little regard for your choices and opinions. Or he may not trust you to do the right thing when you are out of his presence. His underlying motive is to control you and your actions. Think twice because he is attempting to reshape your life.

If your love interest does not spend the time to hear and understand exactly what you are trying to say, he is not interested in your feelings; and therefore, he is not truly interested in you. Something else besides true love is holding him in place, but this is temporary and like shifting sand.

> *"Be happy, young man, while you are young, and let your heart give you joy*
> *in the days of your youth. Follow the ways of your heart*
> *and whatever your eyes see, but know that for all these things,*
> *God will bring you judgment."* (Ecclesiastes 11:9)

If your love interest pouts or yells when you've already conveyed that you know you were wrong about some particular issue or decision, this is a very immature response and may show arrested spiritual development or an inability to forgive and forget. Regardless of what he says, watch his behavior!

Reflection #8: Earning a Living

> *"I have been young, and now I am old, but I have never seen a righteous person*
> *abandoned or his descendants begging for bread."* (Psalm 37:25)

Purpose: An ideal companion should be someone who is already earning a living when you meet him and sees money as a means of reward for solving problems.

Definition. Earning a living may be described as making efforts to earn money legitimately to take care of one's personal and family needs. This is a critical area and should be taken very, very seriously. Lack of money shows some things have not been settled or conquered in this individual. Money is a reward for solving problems. If you never have any money, you are probably refusing to solve the problems nearest you, or for someone else close to you.

> *"But if any provide not for his own, and especially for those of his own house,*
> *he has denied the faith, and is worse than the infidel."* (1 Timothy 5:8)

Defining moments. Money is neither good nor bad, but takes on the personality of its owner. If your love one refuses to find and keep a job, something is terribly wrong. If God is working with an individual through allowing poverty, you cannot rescue him without suffering the consequences. The blessings of the unrighteous are stored up for the righteous – not the other way around. God may then allow poverty in your life so that you cannot help this individual. Or if he is working, but cannot seem to keep money, or pay his bills responsibly, he may have a hidden addiction that takes his money.

A worthy companion should already have the dearest thing to his heart, a reliable car. If he has an auto, is he always running out of gas? Or is it always breaking down? Does he need constant money "favors?"

Your love interest should be self-supporting – his own apartment/home or does he live with mom and dad or someone who helps support him? If you join your life to his, he will just switch supporters from them to you.

> *"She gets up while it is still night; she provides food for her family and*
> *portions for her female servants."* (Proverbs 31:15

You often hear of a man marrying a waitress he met in a small café. Why? He observed her work habits. At three am, she was there bringing pancakes and eggs to truck drivers… with a smile on her face. It was one of the secrets of Solomon. He only hired happy people. It is important to choose a lifetime companion who is already happy and self-supporting before you enter his life.

Paul warned,

> "This we command you, if any would not work, neither should they eat.
> For we hear that there are some who walk amongst you disorderly,

working not at all, but are busybodies…And if any man obey not our word
by this epistle, note that man, and have no company with him, that he
may be ashamed" (2 Thessalonians 3:10-14).

People who are productive energize other people. It's not about class or economics, it about being content and working as unto the LORD and not unto man. (Colossians 3:23)

Reflection #9: Emotional Stability

"These things I have spoken to you so that in me you might have peace.
In the world you shall have tribulations,
but be of good cheer, I have overcome the world." (John 16:33)

Purpose: An ideal companion should be even tempered and not feel inferior to you. They should not make mountains out of molehills; they should be able to differentiate between things that are important and things that are trivial. Check closely to make sure there are no signs of addiction or psychosomatic illness.

Definition. Emotional stability is the capacity to maintain ones emotional balance under stressful circumstances. It may be said to be the quality of being physically or emotionally predictable, orderly, and not easily moved. Emotional stability is an important and useful state of being. When emotions are managed and under control, and yet a man still has the ability to feel intense emotion and understand the reason for his emotions, he has accomplished the power to stand still in situations that cannot be easily shaken or moved. Your emotions serve as a gauge to your inner feelings. If your faith in God is strong, then so will your ability to manage your emotions. Emotions are helpful because they provide additional clarification beyond gut reaction and instinct. Balanced emotions keep us from jumping to conclusions or taking situations into our own hands before seeking counsel from the Holy Spirit.

Defining moments. You should think twice if pebble problems unleash mountains of anger in your love one. This means he cannot differentiate between things that are important and things that are trivial. For example, he shows unreasonable jealousy and anger if someone of the opposite sex calls or says something to you. Or he refuses to stop focusing on or criticizing a mistake long after it is over and done with. Beware. He won't forget; and this can build towards an explosion when a new situation arises.

If he feels inferior to you, he does not feel confident, qualified or called of God to be your lifetime companion. God gave us all different gifts. It is important that those who walk beside you feel they are in their rightful place. The individual who assumes you are more knowledgeable than they, may misunderstand your message, and give up on trying to understand your explanations, or become frustrated or angry because he thinks "you think you are better than me." For example: persons in the preaching and teaching professions are notorious for unintentionally moving into the teaching mode when simply talking to others. If your love one already feels inferior, he may assume you are "insulting his intelligence" or 'talking down' to him rather than understanding that this is just the way you are and mean no disrespect. In this case, he will focus on you and never get your message.

"Let us behave decently, as in the daytime, not in orgies
and drunkenness, not in sexual immorality and debauchery,
not in dissension and jealousy." (Romans 13:13)

Another thing to watch out for is the increasing obsession over cell phones and computers. While they all have their place, if your love one spends inordinate amounts of time on the computer either in or out of your presence, there may be serious attachment problems that will not change over time. Many companions have lived to regret the intense amount of times their mates spend on cell phones and/or computers. Sometimes, the individual may actually be holding foreplay talks. It will be just a matter of time before they will stray time and time again. Even if they do not stray, the computer may be a form of entertainment that replaces quality time with you. (see section on Infidelity).

<u>Signs of Addiction</u>. Are there signs of addiction to drugs, alcohol, pornography, gambling, sex or nicotine? Signs of addiction may come up through inconsistent behavior – lying or stealing to support their addiction. Those addicted have an inverted sleep pattern or spend quality time away from home to hide the effects of the addiction. Many gambling addicts got started playing the lottery. Gambling addicts will have peaks and valleys of money. One day they have lots of money, but more often they are broke because they lost it all gambling. Besides wreaking havoc in everyone's lives, addicts shorten their own lives through stressors and repeated unhealthy assaults on their own bodies.

When a person is addicted, it causes him to be suspicious, unable to receive, unable to give -except in an artificial kind of way. He is fearful both of being exposed and fearful of not being able to function without the source of his addiction. Over a period of time, the reasons why he became addicted may dim and blur. This causes blind spots. The person is no longer able to completely explain why he feels the way he feels or does the things he do. Nor is he able to "see himself" as others see him. He is also more likely to jump to the wrong conclusions. If left untreated, the addict will eventually develop a pseudo personality in order to cope. A pseudo personality is one in which every choice, decision, and feeling is filtered through his need to remain addicted.

Contrary to what you may think, an addicted heart can be a very high functioning individual. He may have a successful career, and may not have any trouble attracting potential spouses. This means the high functioning addicted heart has learned socially acceptable ways of attracting significant others. He may be in a highly successful career in which money is not a problem. But that addicted heart is negatively affecting every circumstance and every relationship (family, marriage, careers, spouse, children, etc.) over a period of time; and under certain stressful conditions, the real person will always begin to seep through.

Therefore, an addicted heart may appear to be a split personality. His private life is the opposite of his professional or public life. To the world, he is charming, successful, healthy and contented. But in private, to his family and close associates and friends, he is anything but. This is why dating over an acceptable period of time and having worthy (impartial) mentors in your life is so important; you will be able to learn more about the habits and moods of an individual and receive objective feedback.

The most critical fact is that an addicted heart is a perfect "set up" to keep this individual from receiving true salvation. *"For God so loved the world, that He sent His only Begotten Son that whosoever will, might receive eternal life"* (John 3:16). An addicted personality is less likely to perceive the love being offered by God – or by others, because of the effects of the addiction. Even if the gospel is preached, they are less likely to accept the love offered by God for fear of exposure. "You mean I have to get up and admit something before all of these people that they know nothing about?" (Or so they believe.) Until he hits rock bottom, he will not understand that God already knows…. And so does everybody else. Being unable to perceive keeps one from truly knowing he is being offered the most precious gift of all, Jesus the Christ, which means eternal life and freedom from the bondage of the addiction.

An even bigger danger to an addicted heart, however, is that it is not impossible for this type of individual to "feel" they have salvation, which leads to self-deception. This self-deception leads to human *doing* for God rather than human *being* in relationship with God.

"Let no man deceive himself. If any man among you seems to be wise in this world, let him become a fool, that he may be wise." (1Corinthians 3:18).

Many make the mistake of believing their presence in the life of an addict will make a difference. They believe they can love and pray the addict out of addiction. While prayer is a good thing, you must remember that the addict has freewill also and God is bound by His own laws. Only a very small percentage of persons end up free of addiction. It is a hard thing to understand for those that are free of addiction, but some actually enjoy their addiction and see no need to change. In that state, they do not recognize the extent of damage they are causing. Since they do not recognize that they are addicted or that addiction is a sin; repentance is not realized. Personal recognition is the prerequisite to confessing and breaking free of addiction.

"That if you shall confess with your mouth the Lord Jesus, and shall believe in your heart that God has raised him from the dead, you shall be saved." (Romans 10:9-10)

If you insist on living your life with someone who is addicted by choice, you will have a miserable life. It will be like committing to going into a big dark hole and possibly never coming out.

Signs of Psychosomatic Illness. When there are signs of psychosomatic illnesses in a love one, seek professional advice for yourself; and then take it. These people are notorious for constantly using the excuse of headaches and physical weaknesses such as stress and chest pains to tug at your emotions and get out of responsibility for their actions. One woman tells the sad story of how her husband habitually went to the hospital emergency room with chest pains after a few consecutive nights out of the home. The hospital would call her and she would go rushing to his side time and time again. Each time he was able to snake his way back into the home with no explanation of his whereabouts for several days because his health took precedence. You will be in a battle that will slowly sap your strength, your sanity and your health.

"So then, banish anxiety from your heart and cast off the troubles of your body, for youth and vigor are meaningless." (Ecclesiastes 11:10)

If your time with your love one always ends with you feeling personal guilt or disappointment, you are already withdrawing from the relationship. Withdrawal always begins with feelings of guilt, fear, or a sense of entrapment. Emotional and psychological withdrawal comes before physical withdrawal. If you remain in the relationship too long, not only will your self-esteem be damaged, which will make it hard for you to move on, but the image of God in you will also be marred. You will forget who God says you are and struggle to go on after the relationship ends.

If your love one does not pamper you when you don't feel well, he does not value your emotional or physical well-being. For instance, if you say "I have a headache," and he immediately starts to tell you he has even worse symptoms than you, or he makes demands on you as if he did not hear you say you are not feeling well, he is trying to convince you that your feelings are nothing compared to what he desires.

"Be sober, be vigilant; because your adversary the devil, as a roaring lion,
walks about, seeking whom he may devour." (1Peter 5:8)

If you have to deal with an addicted or mentally ill companion, your focus will always be about survival. These distractions will cause you to lose sight of other things that should be important – your first love is God; God-centered services, your career, hobbies and your children. If there are too many distractions, which may manifest in worry, anxiety, fear, anger and guilt, then you are in the wrong relationship. If you are so concerned about what he is doing and with whom that you become distant and uncaring about what is going on within other areas of your life (your children's well being, paying bills on time, developing psychosomatic illnesses; you cannot sleep, work or fully enjoying worship in peace, etc.), the person you are with is draining your strength and you may eventually develop a physical illness. Find a way out immediately!

Reflection #10: Family

For this reason I kneel before the Father from whom every family in heave and on earth
derives its name. Ephesians 3:15

<u>Purpose</u>: There are so many sides to all of us. It's not just a matter of "good" or "bad." Perhaps this is most true within our own family. You wear a different hat as a woman depending on your role as a wife, sister, mother, niece, aunt, etc. You may not recognize yourself if you could secretly hear a description of yourself in each of these relationships. The ideal companion should be someone in whom you find refuge and peace, not strife. Your lifetime companion should be someone who gets along well with his family and yours.

Definition. Whoever makes up our family—whether it's our children, parents, spouse, or friends—the feelings we have are often contradictory. Some of our relationships are strained. Some are improving. Feelings change from day to day depending on the love spoken and affirmed. But strife can be avoided – even if it means feeding some out of a long handled spoon. Or waiting for some to "get over" their snits for a time.

Defining moments. Pay attention to how your love one interacts in their own family. This will be a clue as to whether you will be isolated or merged in once the two of you get married. How did your love one chose you as a possible companion? Were they attracted to you as a person? Or to you because you look like someone else they love and admire and will be looking for their attributes in you as well? Was he "talked into" liking you because his family likes you? If so, familiarity may breed contempt once you get together.

Not every person liked their mother while growing up. If your love one starts comparing or calling you their mother's name, be sure and find out why you remind them of their mother. This may not be a compliment.

Also be careful of a mother who talks negatively about her adult children. The steady drip of negative comments will eventually get into your mind and cause you to lose respect for your love one. A mother's opinion of her children is very important to them. Unfortunately, some mothers' hearts have not been regenerated by the Holy Spirit. Their views are worldly and may produce feelings of sadness, low self-esteem and anger in their children. Without the help of God, these emotions will spill over into your relationship with them. Some mothers even advise their children that adultery and cheating in relationship is the "manly thing" to do. Abusive mothers want to control you and your family through controlling the adult son you are married to. Each time he hears negative comments about you, his feelings of love for you are compromised.

"A fraudulent man sows strife, and a whisperer separates chief friends." (Proverbs 16:28)

Think twice if continuous strife exists between him and his parents, or former caretaker. He may not celebrate authority in his life. Honoring our parents was the first commandment with a promise. Those who do not show honor will not heed authority in any other areas of their lives. This means he will not listen to you when the chips are down. This characteristic will cause him to become reactive when he is opposed; and trust me, you won't like it!

Does he make a point of introducing you to his family? The bloodline is more powerful than anyone can imagine. It is a spiritual thing – a spiritual connection. God arranged it Himself.

You may be in a relationship with a rebel, who even despises his own parents, but when crises come, he will reach back to the bloodline for affirmation and help.

If you marry someone whose parents look condescendingly upon you because you lack education, social class, finances or do not meet their godly standards, remember that they will be the third parties always speaking into the heart of your companion. They speak not only orally but through their actions, or lack thereof. If the parents or former caretakers of your love one hold contempt for you, and your assigned goals in life, there may be an eventual eroding of the relationship either with the family or with you.

Reflection #11: Finances

Why do you spend money for what is not bread, and your wages for what does not satisfy? Isaiah 55:2

Purpose: Not everyone is a banking genius; so who will handle the finances should be discussed ahead of time. This does not absolve your love one from working (See "Earning a living") and being productive. An ideal companion should not need to borrow money from other people who might be struggling also. Ask yourself if this individual has money in their pocket from payday to payday. Does he use credit cards successfully? Does he feel the "need" to buy toys? Does he demand spending money on things that he want rather than putting the needs of his family first? Does he believe in frequenting pawn shops that charge high interest? A lot can be gleaned in this area from studying how and where a person lives before joining your life to his. Are they paying their own way or are their parents still supporting them? If so, they will be switching supporters by marrying you.

"For the love of money is the root of all evil: which while some coveted after, they have erred from the faith, and pierced themselves through with many arrows."
(1 Timothy 6:10)

Definition. Finance is the study of funds management. How does your intended lifetime companion feel about and handle money? It is an extremely sensitive and critical area. If you feel you cannot trust the one you wish to marry with your finances, then a marriage with this individual will be like living in a pressure cooker. There will be a continuous struggle to have enough money to pay the bills. You will be looking and double checking bank accounts to see if money is disappearing without your knowledge. This narrows down the field considerably, doesn't it? Do not bond your life with someone too immature to handle the importance of financial responsibility. Empty pockets cannot pay the bills; neither can promises to do better.

Defining moments. You should think about it very carefully if your love one is willing to go into your purse without your permission or seeks ways to obtain money from your bank account without your knowledge. Beware. This individual is revealing that he could care less about how the bills are paid. Are they perfectly at ease about repeatedly asking to borrow money from you or from others? There will be a slow erosion of your ability to meet your obligations. One woman put it this way, "My husband is not interested in how much our bills are each month, only in what new ways he can spend "our" money. Never mind if we can't afford it. Many times I give in to him because he will pout for days if I say we can't afford it. And then I end up calling creditors to rearrange a payment or I end up robbing Peter to pay Paul." How sad. Ungodly advice is usually motivated by the love of money in search of temporary thrills rather than seeking stability.

"Give, and it will be given to you: good measure, pressed down, shaken together and running over will be put in your bosom. For with the same measure you use, it will be measured back to you." (Luke 6:38)

Tithing is good money management. Even if your love one does not tithe, you should tithe because it is a commandment, not an option. Your decision will affect your lifestyle and your household. When we give, we must remember that the blessings God promises are not always material and may not be experienced completely here on earth, but we will certainly receive them in our future life with Him. At any rate, the blessings are for you as well as for your family.

In Acts 3:6 Peter said to the beggar "Silver and gold have I none." If that's what you are looking for, do not look to Christ. He does not promise to those who believe in material gain. Usually it is the poor who listen to the gospel. Faith in Christ does not make them rich with earth's goods, but makes them rich in faith and heirs of the coming kingdom. Money has great value in many ways but it cannot atone for sin, ease sorrow, or relieve suffering. It can buy a fancy tombstone, but it cannot take the sting out of death or cancel divine judgment. Peter had no money, yet he could impart a blessing all the money on earth cannot buy. Like Paul, so Peter – and any believer – can make many rich, though poor in earthly goods. It is great to be God's messenger, with the right to dispense wealth that goes beyond all human calculations. Peter brought this cripple great riches, without becoming poor in doing so. God's grace too is for all, yet makes Him no poorer. In fact, the more we give away of God's money, the greater our store of it becomes.

Secondly, tithing is a clear way to demonstrate our priorities. The Bible makes the purpose of tithing very clear—to put God first in our life. We are to give God the first and best of what we earn. What we do first with our money shows what we value most. Giving the first part of our paycheck to God immediately focuses our attention on Him. It also reminds us that all we have belongs to Him. A habit of regular tithing can keep God at the top of our priority list and give us a proper perspective on everything else we have.

> *"He called His disciple to Him and said, "I assure you, this poor widow has given more than all the others have given. For they gave a tiny part of their surplus, but she, poor as she is, has given everything she has."* (Mark 12:43–44)

Lastly, tithing should remind us of God's desire that we be generous. In the Lord's eyes, this poor widow gave more than all the others put together, though her gift was by far the smallest. The value of a gift is not determined by its amount, but by the spirit in which it is given. A gift given grudgingly or for recognition loses its value. When you give, remember—no matter how small or large your income, your tithe is pleasing to God when it is given out of gratitude and a spirit of generosity.

Reflection #12: Follow Your Dreams

> *"I am the vine; you are the branches. If you remain in me and I in you, you will bear much fruit; apart from me you can do nothing."* John 15:5

Objective: The ideal companion should respect your projects and strivings; your hopes, accomplishments and dreams. They should not feel a need to compete in the relationship. He should be someone who encourages you and is interested in seeing you grow and succeed. He should also have worthy goals himself and be actively following through on them.

Definition. A goal or objective is a desired result that an individual envisions, plans and commits to achieve. It's the manifestation of hidden talents and abilities. The years of our youth quickly pass, and we are soon thrown out into the world, among strangers to provide for ourselves, and we will perhaps have no one to advise us. If we neglect to learn while we have the opportunity, we will be sorry for it in life. If we waste our time in school, we will leave it knowing very little, and an ignorant man can never take any good position in the world; he can seldom be his own master and independent; he must always toil for others as a servant.

> *"He that observes the wind shall not sow, and he that*
> *regards the clouds shall not reap."* (Ecclesiastes 11:4)

Defining moments. God gives us our talents and opportunities that we may use them to the best of our ability to serve His purposes, and He will hold us accountable for these. It is good and praiseworthy to raise ourselves and others in the world if we do so by lawful and proper means. We may have the opportunity of getting a good position, but will not be able to take it if we are not sufficiently educated.

Many young people live to be sorry for wasting time in school, and try to make up for it by studying at night. You cannot really make up for lost time. Every moment God gives you He gives for some particular work, and He will require an account from you, at the last day, for the use you made of your time. Besides, you can learn with greater ease while you are young.

But what shall I say of neglecting salvation? If you neglect your school lessons you will not be successful in the world as a business person or professional; but if you neglect salvation, you will be miserable, not merely in this world, but in the next, and for all eternity. If you bond yourself to such an individual who is not under God's authority, you will inherit their failures. The key here is watching that the dreams of an individual are becoming actualized and not just talk before agreeing to spend the rest of your life with them; for what happens to them will certainly happen to you.

If your love one makes tactless comments about your projects or strivings, he does not value your goals and accomplishments. Or if he does not even notice your accomplishments, he is not concerned about your accomplishments. This may translate into feelings of jealousy or competition, but either way, it means he is not concerned about your goals. The key here is to watch out for these two extreme ways of behaving.

One sure thing is that if he makes fun of your hopes, accomplishments and dreams, there is already competition in the relationship. Ask yourself when good things happen, who is the first person you desire to tell? And how satisfied do you feel after revealing these good things to this individual? How did they respond? Your intended should be able to encourage and motivate you to excellence.

Something is wrong internally if the goals of your love one are not enough to motivate him to excellence. Beware if he talks a lot; seem to have wonderful ideas, but never seem to follow through. Either he has doubts and insecurities about his abilities, or he intends to continuously motivate you to want to stay with him because of his intellect, not his ability or desire to earn a living. The point is it's not about how you feel, but whether he will continuously sabotage the relationship because of how he feels. Look to his reality, not your own.

If your love one makes you feel you haven't tried to improve when you really have, this person does not approve of who you are and what you portray. Whatever attracted him to you in the first place has gone out of the relationship.

You should wonder about humility in him if he does not ask quality questions about your dreams or goals. A humble person is willing to allow someone else to be the center of attention. Asking questions and being willing to help you, reveals a need to get to know you on a deeper level.

Your love one may be draining your strength if he does not motivate you to a higher level of excellence. Everyone has sinned and fallen short of the glory of God, so you already possess weaknesses to be overcome. You do not require anyone to feed them. You can do badly all by yourself. Anyone can pull you down. God will give you a companion to lift you up.

Your love one has a blind spot if he criticizes unjustly. This means he is unable to see the uniqueness in situations or special gifts in each person. Neither will he be able to see your unique gifts and talents.

Reflection #13: Heart Treasures

"Delight yourself in the LORD, and He will Give you the desires and secret petitions of your heart." Psalm 37:4

Purpose: An ideal companion should show interest in and want to participate sometimes in the things that are special to you. They should present you with gifts on special occasions. What do you enjoy? What books do you love to read? Where do you want to go on vacation? What is your favorite movie or song? Your true lifetime companion will want to know these things and more about you.

Definition. Heart treasures may be described as those passionate things that have captured and continue to keep your interest, energy and attention. The Psalmist is talking about the secret petitions of our heart. These are the hidden dreams that you may not have told anybody about. One way you know they must be from God is that they are so big until you know you can only accomplish them with God's help. God does this on purpose so that it will take faith. How big is your faith? Faith is what pleases God. Without faith it is impossible to please God. So God will put a desire in our heart where you don't have the talent, education or resources, the connections or the confidence. God will even allow certain obstacles that we cannot overcome on our own. Remember, God knows exactly where you are and what you need. He's working all things together for His glory and your good.

Defining moments. If you feel your love interest lacks interest in the things that are special to you, you can expect one of two choices. First choice, give up the things that are special to you like church, friends, bible study, thrift store shopping and yard sales, etc.; Or second choice, expect to spend time alone with those special things.

If your love interest gives you the feeling that errors are not in his lifestyle, this individual believes he is perfect. This opinion usually manifests itself in a person who is unwilling to say they are sorry. It may also manifest itself in an individual who is highly critical of you, your goals and of others. He may go so far as to continuously try to tell you or others the "right" thing to say or the "right" way to act, because only he knows the truth. He believes God made a mistake when he put in the Bible that "all" have sinned and fallen short of His Glory" because he should have been excluded. This individual has set a standard so high for others that even he is unable to follow it. Some even use the Bible as a tool to bash others with while being unable to follow its guidelines themselves.

If you feel your love interest continuously dismisses your needs and wants in favor of his own needs & wants, this is a selfish individual who is putting his desires and wants ahead of yours.

Many people forget special occasions, either because they were not introduced to celebration growing up, or because they never took the time to enjoy the moment.

Carelessness in this area may be hard to overcome because it is now an ingrained habit. It is not necessarily the lack of a warm heart. One way to find out whether it is carelessness, or simply "don't care," is to become aware of how he responds to your gift giving. If he derives an incredible amount of joy from receiving, then this individual knows, through the pleasure it brings him, that giving is important.

Your love interest may not be able to show affection if he does not spontaneously hug you when arriving in your presence. This individual may have grown up in a household where affection was seldom displayed. But even so, you "just knew" that others cared for you. However, absence should cause both hearts to grow fonder. This habit or lack of will be hard to overcome.

Reflection #14: Love

"Love is patient, love is kind. It does not envy, it does not boast, it is not proud."
1 Corinthians 13:4

Purpose: An ideal companion should make you feel that you are the center of his universe and what makes him want to wake up in the mornings. Your mate should never be too busy to care for or listen to your needs and wants.

Definition. Love is not just an emotion of strong affection and personal attachment. In philosophical context, love is a virtue representing all of human kindness, compassion, and affection. Love may also be a profoundly tender, passionate affection for another person. It has been described as a feeling of warm personal attachment or deep affection, as for a parent, child, pet or friend. To love or not to love is a decision we weigh very carefully. It should not be based on looks, charm or conversation, but on deliberate and thoughtful weighing of all circumstances involved. Love may easily be mixed up with lust. Beware the act of premarital sex. It may confuse the issue of whether it is true love and make for a very temporary relationship.

Defining moments. Beware the "sensorial fog" brought on when entering into a new relationship. A sensorial fog is the combination of circumstances and feelings that bring about a state of elation, confusion, and exhilaration. What you may be feeling is not necessarily love, but beguilement. The heart is deceptive and may produce a feeling that is hard to decipher from the real thing. Here, worthy mentors should be used to help you remain objective and intentional about what you want to happen in the relationship. The caution here is that a new relationship may beguile our senses, pervert our judgment, and enchant our imagination. If you have not been in a right relationship with worthy mentors all along, it may be hard to use discernment once beguilement has begun.

Young people and young at hearts are cautioned not to belittle the gift of God by allowing "love" to be so easily shown between the sheets. Give the gift of a clean heart to each other, and keep yourselves for each other so that God may always be with you; for a clean heart will always see God. He loves a heart that is totally given over to Him. And my prayer is that you may grow up together in holiness through the love you have one for each other.

If your love interest fails to say "I love you", or show physical affection, unless it is initiated by you, you should wonder what is going on in their head and heart. It could be that your intended was unable to bond with early caretakers; or, may have been wounded by betrayal or lack of affection in the past. They may appear to be whole and healthy, but failure in this area shows they possess a heart that is closed to compassion.

The most important questions you should ask yourself, "Does the Target of my affections have a relationship with God? Are they totally committed to God? In other words, does my intended lifetime companion love the LORD with all his heart, soul, mind and strength?" Be not deceived, a person cannot love self or others if they have not accepted the LORD into their heart. For the Bible tells us that God is love. (1John 4:8,16). In other words, we cannot love others until God comes into our hearts and shows us what love is. God first, then self, then others should be the proper order. Becoming totally committed, therefore, is learning to listen to God's inner voice as He guides you.

Reflection #15: Maintenance

"Wives submit to your husbands, as is fitting in the LORD. Husbands, love your wives."
(Colossians 3:18-19)

Purpose: There should be continuous improvement in the relationship and a decrease in conflict over time. Companions should experience increasing closeness and a need to be around one another. Your intended should long to pleasure you through gift giving, a need to get away and be just with each other and by saying "I Love You" often in words and deeds.

Definition. Maintaining the **r**elationship may be described as continuous interpersonal actions and communications between two people that increase enduring affection.

Defining moments. Obviously, God loves every one of us regardless of our sin. However, anything that grieves the Holy Spirit should grieve us. Anything that angers God should anger us. Anything that saddens God should sadden us. If you insist on having a relationship with someone who is comfortable with rebellion, stubborn, and arrogant, you will eventually be heartbroken.

If they sneer at the law of God, belittle preachers, and think that holy living is a joke, they are living in defiance of God. It will be impossible to have a Godly relationship with them.

Appearances do count. Physical appearance, dress, grooming, posture, presence, and poise either underscore his need to impress you or his lack thereof. So does his behavior.

If he has lost the desire to impress you, then he has lost that first blush of excitement at an impending meeting with you. He no longer feels it important for you to see him dressed up. He takes no special pains to look nice or smell good; no sense of exciting anticipation crosses his mind when he thinks of you. He is a walking message system to you. He either looks the part of someone who wants to be in the relationship, or he looks the part of a person who is trapped and attempting to force the other person to leave through observing visibly damaged goods in him. Something is terribly wrong when he no longer desires to act and look his best for you. You should be the most special person in his life. Opening doors and allowing you to go in ahead of him are little things that say a lot.

If your love one does not possess a passionate desire to give to you, your love one already feels trapped and wants out of the relationship. This person is trying to force you to make the first move. I am not referring to expensive gifts, large amounts of money, clothes, cars, etc. But uncommon love requires uncommon gifts: a listening ear, flexibility, patience, and a biggie: the willingness to be corrected. The proof of love is the desire to give. Jesus explained it this way:

"For God so loved the world that He gave His only Begotten Son …" John 3:16.

Sad to say but some relationships exist because of a feeling of commitment to some organization, or out of desperation or loneliness. Do you have the feeling that you are more like his sister than a worthy companion? If there are nagging doubts about your love one during your moments of strength, you really don't want to be in relationship with this individual. You feel vulnerable or weak around them. The longer you wait to face this fact, the harder it will become to get out.

If it is obvious that you will never become the major focus in the relationship, you are in the wrong relationship. Your love one may enjoy you; laugh with you, and even like you. They may be truly trustworthy as a confidant, but a person who qualifies for your attention, does not always qualify as a lifetime companion. When God brings you a lifetime companion, that person becomes your mentor. Many marriages are fragmented. Good men and women are often in miserable marriages. Publicly, their life looks glamorous and exciting. Many are even famous and well known. But they despise their marriage because they have ceased to view the other as the true love of their life.

Reflection #16: A Matter of Patience

"He that walks uprightly walks surely; but he that perverts his ways shall be known."
(Proverbs 10:9)

Purpose: An ideal mate should have a measure of patience with you, understanding that God is not finished with you yet. Patience is a fruit of the Spirit. (Galatians 5:22)

Definition. It you are at the beginning or in the middle of a relationship, it would be wise to bring the one you wish to marry with you into the presence of God. If your intended is unwilling to come before God in worship and prayer, what does that say about your future with him? Even if he is willing at the beginning, only time can tell whether he is sincere.

Defining moments. Don't be in too big of a hurry to make a lifetime decision. Time will reveal things that will help you to be in a better position to decide if this is someone you want to spend the rest of your life with.

Take a moment to sit down and assess your present relationship honestly and clearly. Where do you stand? This is one in which we are more likely to procrastinate because what we may suspect is too painful for us to actively seek to get a clear answer to. However, with time the answer will emerge whether you want it to or not. It's just a matter of time. It is better to know sooner than to find out later, after you have invested so much of yourself into the relationship.

Never lean to your own understanding. God already knows more about you and your love one than either of you will ever know about each other, or yourselves. It would be wise to stay in the presence of God, ask Him whether the one you wish to marry is in His plans for you. Ask Him to give you the strength to accept His answer. Be prepared to move on if God's answer is no. Understand that His no in this relationship, will be a yes to another relationship that is just waiting for you.

Recognition of a Godly lifetime companion will bring you years of joy, enthusiasm, and fulfillment because God will be in charge of the relationship. But making the wrong choice will bring you a companion who is does not believe in being under God's authority. You may have the same amount of years, but with tears, heaviness and a sense of regret and emptiness.

Reflection #17: Opposite Sex, the

"Wives, be subject to your husbands, as is fitting in the Lord. Husbands, love your wives and do not be embittered against them." Colossians 3:18-19

Purpose: An ideal companion should be someone who does not need you to constantly reassure him that you love him and need him. Your ideal companion should be someone who does not possess a wandering eye for the opposite sex and one who feels self-assured as far as his worthiness to be your mate is concerned. He should not feel a need to brag or constantly talk about past conquests.

Definition. For our purposes, the opposite sex may be described as any past or present individual that your love one has made or is now making intense, though fleeting attempts to gain the attention of for romantic purposes.

Defining moments. If your love one feels a need for constant reassurance and attention from the opposite sex, this individual is immature. He may not be capable of making the choice to choose loyalty to a relationship with you, or anyone else. Some people are unhappy unless every person of the opposite sex gravitates towards them and they are the center of attraction. Some people cannot pass a mirror without stopping to admire their own perceived attractiveness. *"A discerning person keeps wisdom in view, but a fool's eyes wander to the ends of the earth."* (Proverbs 17:24)

If your love one brags to you about their past conquests and tries to make you feel sorry that temptation to the opposite sex is a continuing struggle for them, your intended is admitting that there is a lack of self-control and warning you that a relationship with them will always result in third, fourth and fifth party involvements. Take them seriously!

Flirtation is dangerous. The death of many relationships began with flirtation. It is never harmless. If you feel you cannot trust your love one around your closest friends, you need to examine why you feel this way? Is it you, or has your love one done something to deserve your distrust?

If he keeps bringing up old mistakes from the past to deal with present problems, he is comparing what has been to what is, and is unable to move into new possibilities and the future, perhaps because of fear of the law of repetition or because he fails to see your uniqueness.

If you feel he fails to celebrate your presence in his life, you can look to eventually be replaced, or have him wander to someone else.

Reflection #18: Respect

"Nevertheless, let everyone of you in particular so love his wife even as himself; and the wife see that she reverence her husband." (Ephesians 5:33)

Purpose: An ideal companion should be someone who does not take you for granted; who expresses respect when he is alone or in the presence of others. He should show a willingness to obey generally accepted social rules and put your needs ahead of his own.

Definition. Respect denotes both a positive feeling of self-esteem for a person and also specific actions and conduct that indicates sensitivity to the feelings and needs of others; and a willingness to obey generally accepted social rules, and claim no right or desire to prosper at the others' expense.

Defining moments. If your love one treats the favor of others with ingratitude, he does not value the gift. A friend of mine once said 'I simply wasn't taught to say I love you. It should be enough that I'm with you." Tares! If he never acknowledges gifts or says "thank you," it's an indication that he does not value it or the giver. However, as with forgetting special occasions, if you feel these are learned behaviors, he will be hard to change. Attempting to correct may cause him to feel you are being too critical. You can't punish anyone into being thoughtful. You can, however, model thoughtful behaviors. Here, showing by example will be the best way to proceed. Or using "I" statements, such as "I can't tell that you like what I did for you," may be an efficient method of leading by example.

When someone loves you, he will admire your achievements. He will want to hear you more than talk about his own accomplishments. Have you mastered prejudice, fears, or poverty? If your love one shows little respect for battles you've already won in your lifetime, he does not respect or value your accomplishments.

Your love one has too high of an importance of his own self-worth, if he is perpetually late for meetings and appointments, or gives excuses not to attend. If you feel he shows little respect for the agenda and schedule of others, he is inconsiderate of other people's time.

Your love one should seek your opinion before making major decisions that affect you. If he continues to make major decisions in life without pursuing your opinion, your opinion is neither wanted nor needed.

If your love one misunderstands your motives, this is a sign of distrust. Distrust may be deeply embedded in some past experience he has had. Or, he may not have forgiven you for some past act you have committed. A third reason could be that he may have embraced some gossip about you.

Your love one is either unable or unwilling to forgive, if he continues to try to punish you after you've asked for forgiveness. His behavior belies his confession, even if he says he has forgiven you.

If he tells you verbally or by his actions that your opinions do not matter, he doubts your ability to make correct or wise decisions.

Your intended is insensitive to your feelings or self-centered if he lacks understanding at times when all you need is his support. A self-centered individual is so busy taking care of his own needs until he is unable to sympathize with or allow another into his inner circle.

Reflection #19: Spending Quality Time Together

"Likewise, you husbands, dwell with them according to knowledge, giving honor to the wife, as to the weaker vessel, and as being heirs together of the grace of life; that your prayers be not hindered." (1 Peter 3:7)

Purpose: The ideal companion should want to spend as much quality time alone with you as is possible; he should want to get to know you and have you get to know him. He should be considerate of your feelings and plan his schedule around yours.

Definition. Quality time is different from just being around one another. Quality time means attending to the needs of the other; listening and being fully present in body, mind and spirit, and giving the other your advice and feedback about something they may be struggling with. It also means seeking time to date and keep the relationship fresh and exciting.

Defining moments. If your love one fails to spend quality time alone with you, when there is a choice, you are being denied one of the benefits of the relationship. He may be hiding something and fear he may be exposed if he spends too much time with you.

If he shows inconsideration for you as a thinking, feeling human being, you may simply be valuable to him on a temporary basis or because of something you have to offer that he cannot do without (business agreement, finances, etc.).

The bottom line is if the one you wish to marry shows over a period of time that he is too busy to care for or listen to you, he does not value your presence or your opinion.

Reflection #20: Trust

Her husband has full confidence in her and lacks nothing of value.
(Proverbs 31:11)

Purpose: The ideal companion should be someone you can trust with your most painful memories; someone who will use discretion and build you up rather than tear you down. It should be someone who will not easily embrace gossip about you and is willing to be comforted by you as well.

Definition. Trust may be described as a firm reliance on the integrity, strength, ability, surety, etc. of a person; confidence. If you feel you cannot trust the one you wish to marry with your most painful memories, your heart is closed to revealing your innermost struggles and desires to this person and something else is holding you in place. Every person is running from painful memories. Many adults share that their childhood was filled with pain. People of excellence often share that their days of poverty have motivated them to do better. Their painful memories have driven them to uncommon achievement. Some explain a father or mother who beat them unmercifully. All of us have childhood memories that are painful, shameful and often unbearable. Listening to memories are the keys to understanding another person.

Defining moments. If you cannot trust the one you wish to marry to empathize with your memories, neither will he be able to understand who you truly are.

Fear is the opposite of trust and often limits us. Trust should be inspiring and motivate us to higher limits. It may be the fear of flying, or fear of the dark. It may be a fear of dying with disease. Whatever it is, love should be strong enough to destroy fear. *"Perfect love casts out fear."* (1John 4:18) You should feel that you can trust him with your greatest fears or secrets. You should not feel afraid that he may stop loving you if you expose yourself to him.

The weaknesses of a very important relationship will be exposed when the other flies into a rage and starts to question you intensely about the details of an accusation. Lack of loyalties will be identified and exposed eventually if you feel he is quick to embrace an accusation against you. If he never assumes that those around him might be lying or misinformed – no matter how close, you are dealing with a reflector rather than a reflective, credible thinker. How can he have arrived at a credible final opinion or decision about you if he has not taken time for thorough consideration? Truth may not be his focus and your opinion may not be important.

It may be heartbreaking to realize that your relationship may be very fragile if others can lie about you and your explanation would never be valued or believed. If you feel either you or he has unresolved issues in this area, the relationship is in trouble at its very root. Jealousy is a cruel dictator and tyrant. It is often unfounded and produced by a painful memory of disloyalty or betrayal in the past. A lot of relationships have unraveled because of a deep sense of distrust. Pay attention to the signals. Trusting God must come before we can trust others.

If you feel you cannot trust them with the knowledge of your greatest weakness, you are not willing to allow him into your private place. Each of us contains weaknesses that embarrass us. We despise them. All have fallen short of the glory of God. It may be anger, fear or lust. Your significant other should be there to strengthen you. If you believe it is necessary to hide your weakness instead of sharing it, you have the wrong aim and the wrong companion.

If you feel your love continuously builds you up and then lets you down, this individual is manipulating you and will say and promise whatever it takes at the moment, with no intentions of following through. If this individual continuously gets your hopes up, but fails to follow through, he is a liar; and you are on a roller coaster, and need to get off immediately!

CHAPTER X

Dancing Through the Storms: Learning to Live Confidently in a Chaotic World

"Suddenly, a violent storm arose on the sea, so that the boat was being swamped by the waves. But He was sleeping." Matthew 8:24

It should be of great comfort to all of us who have surrendered to Christ, and have His many promises, that we have a Savior we can put our trust in and pray to; One who knows what it is like to be in the storms of life. We have a God who can sympathize with us because He was in the world as a man and was tempted as we are. Christ came to show us the way. He said without Me, you can do nothing. Christ was talking about the Believer's access to the Holy Spirit to lead and guide and help us make the best decisions – not always the most popular ones. In other words, we have spiritual tools that are not available to the world.

We have a God who is full of compassion and His mercies endure forever. If we seek to gain the mind of Christ, we must develop a greater heart of compassion. "Lord forgive them for they know not what they are doing." Luke 23:34

Those who are passing with Christ over the land of life must expect storms. His human nature, like ours got tired; He wept with sorrow, He got hungry and He slept at this time to try the faith of His disciples. And your faith will be tried.

The disciples, in their fear, came to their Master. So it must be in our soul; when lusts and temptations are swelling and raging, and God seems to be asleep to our needs, we may oftentimes be brought to the brink of despair. Then we must go to our Master and cry out in prayer for a word from his mouth, "Lord Jesus, speak to my heart; let me know what I should do. If not, I cannot make it alone." And then, having prayed, believe that He hears and will answer you. Not in your timing, but in His.

Many times, even when we have true faith, we are weak in it. As Christ's disciples we are apt to be disquieted with fears in a stormy day; Storms come to torment us that things are bad with us; God is not with us; and that things will get worse.

When great storms of doubt and fear wash over our soul, under the power of the spirit of bondage, we must believe it will end in a wonderful calm, created and spoken by the Spirit of adoption. The disciples were astonished. They never saw a storm so turned at once into a perfect calm. He that can do this can do anything, which encourages confidence and comfort in Him, in the stormiest day – whether the storm is within or without.

If you keep an open spirit and walk in the ways of the LORD, He will continually reveal to you mysteries thru trials and blessings thru obedience which will both amaze and delight you. He will cause you to dance thru the storms as you become aware of God's constant presence and unconditional love in your life! May God cause you to abound in mercy towards one another…

Angling as an Analogy to Dating

"Strength and honor are her clothing; and she shall rejoice in time to come."
Proverbs 31:25

As a single woman, I want you to imagine that God wants to make you a fisher of men, not the other way around! In order to be a fisher, you must understand certain rules of the game. First, the number one rule to be successful in any endeavor is "Godliness with contentment is great gain." (1 Timothy 6:6)

Godliness has to do with our state of mind and how we conduct ourselves. Contentment comes from using discretion and correctly judging all things. Another way of putting it is learning how to live a God centric life through following our inward witness – the Holy Spirit. Being led by the Holy Spirit means putting first the things of the Kingdom of God. God will never lead you wrong. He will talk with you, walk with you and reveal to you what you ask of Him (James 1:5). You cannot properly discern true love until you are convinced of God's love for you. Only when you need Him more than you need to breathe, will you be qualified to properly love and join your life with another.

A Roll of the Dice. It is extremely important that you choose someone who already possesses humility or a willingness to listen to and heed wise counsel. Otherwise, there is little chance of forming a lasting, harmonious relationship with this individual. They will challenge you every step of the way.

No matter how much discernment you may have or experience from your own life, each love interest is new and exciting. A budding relationship makes one feel positively intoxicated. "This time, whatever has happened to others will not happen to me." Finding the right lifetime companion should not be left up to a chance meeting at a chance time and a chance place. The dangers of entering into an abusive relationship are too great and may cause a lifetime of pain and missed opportunities not only for that spouse, but for any children that are brought into the union. Change your focus and change your future.

Certainly, there are many true romances that end well; and I applaud them! But I believe romantic love is not enough to sustain a relationship over the long haul. In the throes of budding love, we are liable to make emotional decisions based on feelings that are not objective enough. Women should be alerted to what might happen in the wrong relationship. If she is well informed, she will be in a better position to weed out a potentially bad boy who may try to form a bond with her. Keep your feet firmly planted on the ground.

Second, **you** must see your position while you are fishing for the right relationship. Angling in the sense in which I am using it means using godly **tenacity** (a firmness to hold fast; stubbornness; persistence; the ability to remember under tough and oftentimes hostile circumstances who you are and who God is in your life), to construct an image of yourself as a child of God and know what you are willing to tolerate in a relationship (no less than what God says you are entitled to). When you choose to tolerate the behaviors of someone, you choose the accompanying consequences. We all have a personal truth that we feel about our self-worth. We generate that truth in what we are willing to put up with on a job, in a marriage, from our families, you name it. Once you commit yourself in a relationship, your next step is to bloom in the relationship that you've planted yourself in. The balance is to make sure your choice is also God's choice for you.

In this tenacious position, you are not helpless, allowing yourself to drift and be caught by just anyone. You are the fisher standing on the bank or in a boat—not in the murky waters of life. The murky water could represent pollution through contact, or just obscurity from not using discernment to see what otherwise is unknown to you. In other words, you must become hyper vigilant; searching out not only the hearts of men, but discerning ahead of time what environment would be created by joining your life to another– and how this relationship will impact future children that may be brought into the relationship.

Third, you must understand that the rules on the bank are different from the rules in the water. In other words, the fish's rules (the world of men) are different from the Angler's rules (world of women). As the Angler, you are in charge of the pole and the angling. From this position, you operate in strength. It's important to have a clear view of what is being drawn towards you once it is out of the murky water and has captured your attention. Some fish are dangerous, some are beautiful, but they don't all have the same thoughts/motives in mind. You will not always be able to distinguish and weed out by outward appearances which are compulsive flirts or commitment phobic or self-absorbed seducers or wounded poets or the Prince of Darkness. But from your vantage point on the shore, you can decide to keep or throw back whatever is caught.

Dating is like this. Some people's lifestyle will not mesh with whatever lifestyle God wants to create for you. You must search out the heart of a love interest thoroughly through words and actions as you get to know an individual. [Sex too early will complicate the issues.]

Art of Communicating for Positive Results

"Let your conversation be always full of grace, seasoned with salt, so that you may know how to answer everyone." Colossians 4:6

"Don't use foul or abusive language. Let everything you say be good and helpful, so that your words will be an encouragement to those who hear them." Ephesians 4:29

"It's not right that dirty stories, foolish talk, or obscene jokes should be mentioned among you either. Instead, give thanks [to God]." Ephesians 5:4

"A gentle answer turns away wrath, but a harsh word stirs up anger." Proverbs 15:1

When you are in conversation, regardless of the circumstances, you must be committed to managing your own conversation style to foster a Christ-like atmosphere. Someone else's lack in this area does not excuse you. They may not be as skilled in this area and you must continue to follow the Lamb of God's advice. To this end, always pray for understanding if possible before beginning a difficult conversation. Here are some more Christ-like rules to aid your spiritual growth in this area:

1) Commit to speak and live by HEART Principles.
   Hear and understand the other.
   Even if you disagree, please don't make the other bad or wrong.
   Acknowledge the importance of the other in God's sight.
   Remember to *look for* positive intentions, not bad.
   Tell the truth with compassion.

2) Seek win–win solutions to problems, conflicts or any other issues that arise.
3) Keep agreements, and stay open and honest in communications.
4) You should assume 100 percent responsibility for the results that are being produced during the conversation. No blaming, calling names, or justifying.
5) Understand what can happen when you **do not** follow Heart Rules:
   - Diverts attention, time and energy from the main issues
   Obstructs the exploration of other alternatives
   - Creates deadlocks
   - Decreases sensitivity
   Arouses anger and hard feelings
   - Interferes with listening
   - Causes other members not to want to come or participate

Become Spiritually Mature

"Wisdom is the principal thing; therefore get wisdom:
and with all your getting get understanding." Proverbs 4:7

To have a successful relationship – in any area, you must become spiritually mature. Spiritual maturity requires wisdom and the necessary balance to rightly divide the Word and apply it to every situation. When God commissioned Joshua, He told him not to look to the right or to the left, but only to the Word (Joshua 1:7). Any of us long time Christians may find ourselves victims of what appears to be arrested spiritual development; meaning stuck and going round and round the same issues day after day and year after year.

"When I was a child, I used to speak like a child, think like a child, reason like a child;
when I became a man, I did away with childish things." 1 Corinthians 13:11

Despite the length of time we have been converted, we seem no farther ahead than when we first came to know Christ. We continue to throw temper tantrums and find it impossible to keep a lid on our anger. We still demonstrate faithlessness, jealousy, lust and a myriad other works of the flesh (Galatians 5:19). At the same time, we display precious little of the fruit of the Spirit (Galatians 5:22 ff.). In rare moments of introspection we may wonder, "What have I done with all of these years? I seem as carnal today as when I started this Christian journey!" We may even question the validity of our own conversion. Am I really saved? Is God pleased with me?

In a way, the very willingness to ask such questions is itself an indicator of at least "some" spiritual growth. It takes a degree of maturity and humility to recognize and acknowledge one's spiritual shortcomings. If you find yourself thinking this way from time to time, you're probably on the right path. None of us should ever be satisfied with the state of our spirituality. We should be seeking to grow closer, wiser, onward, upward and to stay on fire for God.

On the other hand, those who believe that they are already spiritually mature are in some trouble. None of us is as mature in the faith as we ought to be – at least not when measured by the standards of Jesus Christ.

For many Christians, spiritual maturity is elusive. It is something they know they should aim for, yet they have no idea how to achieve it. The key indicator of spiritual maturity is one's ability to love in a godly way. How do we know this? To be spiritually mature is to be like God. We have been called to imitate God. Paul wrote to the Ephesians:

"Be imitators of God, therefore, as dearly beloved children and live a life of love, just as
Christ loved us and gave Himself up for us as a fragrant offering and sacrifice to God."
(Ephesians 5:1-2)

The apostle John wrote, *"Whoever does not love does not know God, because God is love."* (1John 4:8). To know and be like God is to have developed a capacity for godly love. The Spirit of God influences us to love. It stands to reason then that the more of the Holy Spirit we have, the greater will be our capacity and inclination to love in a godly manner. Paul wrote:

"And hope does not disappoint us, because God has poured out his love into our hearts
by the Holy Spirit, whom He has given us." (Romans 5:5)

Of course, there are those who ridicule the notion that Christians should express love in an emotional way. They view it as mere temporary hype. They make fun of Christians – especially men – who openly express affection through hugging, verbal expression, or emotion. Several years ago, a woman who was a neighbor of one of my late relatives expressed repulsion at the fact that men at the local Church openly hugged each other right out on the street in front of the Church! She seemed to believe that the church was encouraging, contrary to Scripture, homosexual relationships between men.

This well-meaning lady had no clue about the power of God. In her mind, she was expressing righteous indignation, and the men were expressing perversion! She couldn't have been more wrong. Yet, her life to date had been a story of good works and care for others. She could understand love so long as it was expressed in an unemotional way.

What is NOT Spiritual Maturity?

- Being a church member for years
- Having Intimate knowledge of your church's doctrines.
- Going to services every week.
- Being elderly
- Having a loud voice and domineering personality.
- Having relatives that are church leaders.
- Spending time with church leaders
- Being financially well-off or owning a business
- Giving significant sums of money to the church

- Being a great preacher.
- Being good at putting other people down
- Being a deacon or "ordained"

- Being high up in the church's hierarchical structure
- Knowing a lot about the Bible
- Dressing well to go to church

<u>What was Jesus' New Commandment?</u>

Jesus, in teaching His own disciples, said,

> *"A new command I give you: Love one another. As I have loved you, so you must love one another. By this all men will know that you are my disciples, if you love one another"* (John 13:34–35).

Now ask yourself this: If Jesus' disciples did not openly express their love for each other, then how would "all men" know that they were his followers? Therefore, community is important to our spiritual maturity. Of course the issue is how was this affection and love appropriately expressed? There truly were occasions in which the disciples of Jesus showed physical affection for each other, like when John leaned against Jesus' breast to ask Him who would betray Him:

> *"One of them, the disciple whom Jesus loved, was reclining next to him … Leaning back against Jesus, he (John) asked Him, 'Lord, who is it?'"* John 13:23

The way the first Christians treated each other in public was the visible sign that they were Christians. Their interpersonal relationships were wholesome, selfless, giving, forgiving, and mutually supportive. Unlike much of the Church today, they were not competitive enemies. They were "in it together." At the same time, they had their occasional disagreements. After appropriate prayer and haggling, they worked out their differences and moved in unison ahead (i.e. Acts 15).

Love, like faith, without works or manifestation, is dead. If we say we have love, but we do nothing that demonstrates it, we have no reason to claim it. Love, to be love, has to have arms and legs. The word **love** in the New Testament is translated from the Greek word *agapao*. This word is *Strong's Concordance* #G25, which is the root for the Greek word **agape** (*Strong's Concordance* #G26). Nothing in the Greek-English Lexicon suggests that it means primarily a display of emotion or affection, yet that need not be excluded. In short,

Jesus taught that if one is a true Christian, one loves one's fellow Christians. How this love is manifested is determined by the need of the moment.

Love is the antonym for hate. True Christians do not hate other Christians for any reason. If they do so, it is a symptom of spiritual immaturity. It is one thing to disagree on a point or issue, it is quite another to hate. There is no room in the Christian's emotional vocabulary for hatred.

Arrested spiritual development? The apostle Paul was concerned for the spiritual maturity of the churches under his care. In reflecting on his own spiritual development, Paul wrote to the Corinthians, *"When I was a child, I talked like a child; I thought like a child, I reasoned like a child. When I became a man, I put childish things behind me" (1Corinthians 13:11).*

*Con*sider the nature of a child. The smaller the child, the more self-centered it tends to be. A small baby thinks only of its own needs, comfort and wants. It is a black hole of self, sucking everything into it. It sees the universe as revolving around itself.

As the child grows, its awareness of things, people and needs outside of itself is heightened. Instead of seeing all toys as its own, it eventually learns that some toys belong to other children. Gradually, incrementally, the child's world opens up. As it matures, it moves progressively outside of itself into the larger world of others. Over time, it becomes "socialized."

Children who freeze their emotional and intellectual progress at certain levels are said to have become victims of arrested development. We have all know adult men and women who appear to be emotional adolescents. Such people can become "emotional vampires" sucking the energy of all who come in contact with them. Like children, they use emotion as a weapon. Sometimes such arrested adults use "emotional blackmail" techniques to manipulate and control others. Books have been written on this subject.

If an arrested or immature adult is not getting enough attention, he or she may, like a neglected child, seek "negative strokes" by doing something outrageous, creating a crisis, or accusing someone close of something of which they are not guilty. Now all attention shifts to the person generating the crisis. Everyone around them begins to appease and cater to the proverbial "squeaky wheel." Some react defensively.

Either that or they become angry with them. The troublemaker now has what he or she wanted: attention and control. Such arrested people would rather receive negative attention than to be ignored. Every family it seems has in it a gaggle of such people. They test the maturity of all of the other family members. They challenge us, stretch us, and force us to dig deep into our bag of emotional and spiritual resources. They try our patience to the max. Often they drive us to our knees in prayer.

The problem of arrested development occurs in people at both the natural level and at the spiritual level.

Gray hair is generally thought of as a sign of maturity and wisdom. The Bible teaches that not only do those with gray hair deserve respect but it is also a "**crown of glory**" to those who are spiritually mature:

"You shall rise before the GRAY HEADED and honor the presence of an old man, and fear your God: I am the Lord." (Leviticus 19:32, NKJV)

"The SILVER-HAIRED HEAD is a crown of glory, if it is found in the way of righteousness." (Proverbs 16:31, NKJV)

TESTS for arrested spiritual development: When we find Christians who have been baptized for decades behaving as though they were "baby Christians," we are probably looking at cases of arrested spiritual development. If we find ourselves fighting the same old problems we fought when we were first converted, we may be suffering from it ourselves.

Ways of testing for arrested spiritual development:

- Do you still have just as big a problem with your temper as when you were first converted?
- Do you feel spiritually powerless?
- Do you have long dry spells in which nothing seems to be going on between you and God?
- Are you unable to generate love, care and concern for others?
- Do you live a fundamentally self-centered, self-seeking life?
- Do you still seek to manipulate and control others through tantrums and other negative techniques?
- Do anger, hatred and jealousy play an inordinately large role in the way you express your personality?
- Do you put others down to make yourself look better?
- Does your life reflect more of the works of the flesh than fruit of the Spirit?

If you are honest, these questions and their answers are revealing. They can be helpful in taking stock of where you are in a trajectory toward spiritual maturity.

Command Your Morning

"Have you commanded the morning since your days and caused the dawn to know its place?" Job 38:12

An important part of ordering your day is rising early to seek the Lord through prayer. We should also speak to Him each night before we go to sleep. God wants to speak into your life so that He can help you order your day with greater authority and success. There are many problems that come to bear us down and bear down our loved ones. We are to be intercessors; praying for those who are unable to pray for themselves. We are to pray until there is a shift in the atmosphere and strongholds are broken. Tap into God's best for you by rising early to spend time in His presence; and having your last thoughts of Him before you lie down to rest.

"Yes, by my spirit within me I will seek you early; for when Your judgments are in the earth,
The inhabitants of the world will learn righteousness." Isaiah 26:6

Let the LORD fill your heart with His peace and joy, stand firm on His promises that He has good plans for you, and get His special word for you so that you can stand and declare it throughout the day. Seek wisdom; rise early, as did the prophet Isaiah, so that you will have the tongue of the wise, ready to give an answer for the hope that is in you.

"He spake a parable unto them that men ought to always pray, and not faint.
Luke 18:1

No temptation in the life of intercession is more common than this of failure to persevere. We begin to pray for a certain thing: we put up our petition for a day, a week, a month: and then, receiving as yet no definite answer, straightway we faint, and cease altogether from prayer concerning it.

This is a deadly fault. It is simply the snare of many beginnings with no completions. It is ruinous in all spheres of life.

The woman who forms the habit of beginning without finishing has simply formed the habit of failure. The woman who begins to pray about a thing and does not pray it through to a successful issue of answer has formed the same habit in prayer.

To faint is to fail; then defeat begets disheartenment and unfaith in the reality of prayer, which is fatal to all success.

But someone says, "How long shall we pray? Do we not come to a place where we may cease from our petitions and rest the matter in God's hands?"

There is but one answer. Pray until the thing you pray for has actually been granted, or until you have the assurance in your heart that it will be.

Only at one of these two places dare we stay our importunity, for prayer is not only a calling upon God, but also a conflict with Satan. And inasmuch as God is using our intercession as a mighty factor of victory in that conflict, He alone, and not we, must decide when we dare cease from our petitioning. So we dare not stay our prayer until the answer itself has come, or until we receive the assurance that it will come.

In the first place we stop because we see. In the other, we stop because we believe, and the faith of our hearts is just as sure as the sight of our eyes; for it faith from, yes, the faith of God, within us.

More and more, as we live the prayer life, shall we come to experience and recognize this God-given assurance, and know when to rest quietly in it, or when to continue our petitioning until we receive it.

Tarry at the promise till God meets you there. He always returns by way of His promises.

"Likewise the Spirit also helps our infirmities: for we know not what we should pray
for as we ought: but the Spirit itself makes intercession for us with groanings which
cannot be uttered." Romans 8:26

Much that perplexes us in our Christian experience is but the answer to our prayers. We pray for patience, and our Father sends those who tax us to the utmost; for "tribulation worketh patience." Romans 5:3

We pray for submission, and God send sufferings; for "we learn obedience by the things we suffer."

We pray for unselfishness, and God gives us opportunities to sacrifice ourselves by thinking on the things of others, and by laying down our lives for the brethren.

We pray for strength and humility, and some messenger of Satan torments us until we lie in the dust crying for its removal.

We pray, LORD, increase my faith," and money takes wings; or the children are alarmingly ill; or a servant comes who is careless, extravagant, untidy or slow, or some hitherto unknown trial calls for a increase of faith along a line wherever have not needed to exercise much faith before.

We pray for the Lamb-life, and are given a portion of lowly service, or we are injured and must seek no redress; for "he was led as a lamb to the slaughter and … opened not his mouth."

We pray for gentleness, and there comes a perfect storm of temptation to harshness and irritability. We pray for quietness, and every nerve is strung to the utmost tension, so that looking to Him we may learn that when He gives quietness, no one can make trouble.

We pray for love, and God sends peculiar suffering and puts us with apparently unlovely people, and lets them say things which rasp the nerves and lacerate the heart; for love suffers long and is kind, love is not impolite, love is not provoked. Love bears all things, believeth, hopes and endures, love never fails.

We pray for likeness to Jesus, and the answer is, "I have chosen thee in the furnace of afflictions." Can your heart endure, or can your hands be strong?" "Are ye able?" 1 Corinthians 3:2

The way to peace and victory is to accept every circumstance, every trial, straight from the hand of a loving Father; and to live up in the heavenly places, above the clouds, in the very presence of the throne, and to look down from the glory upon our environment as lovingly and divinely appointed.

Confess the Word!

"… even God, who gives life to the dead and calls into being that which does not exist." (Romans 4:17)

When my husband was still running around in the streets, God helped me understand the meaning of the Scripture that "while we were yet sinners, Christ died for the ungodly" (Romans 5:6). Because my husband was not saved, he did not have the indwelling of the Holy Spirit to help him resist temptation. His inner struggles were affecting me and his family, but I did not need to take it personally but pray for his salvation.

As his wife, I could allow the power of the Holy Spirit to develop in me the ability to be joyful in hope, patient in affliction, faithful in prayer (Romans 12:12) At first, my prayers vacillated from asking God to protect my husband to asking him to do him harm depending on circumstances and how I was feeling. Then one day, God spoke to me. "He's my child too, just like you are. I am working it out for Him just like I am working it out for you." I realized that I was building up then tearing down through my mouth. What did I want? Until I decided, God couldn't bless me; nor answer my prayers.

I finally realized I should speak positive things into my life because God honors His word. I began calling my husband a man of God (and adding when it was necessary that he just didn't know it yet). Eventually he heard me and decided to believe me when he saw me trying to live up to this positive point of view. Eventually, He walked down the aisle and gave his life to God.

After my husband was born again, I witnessed a most marvelous thing – his walk of spiritual faith paralleled closely his natural birth. He had to learn how to use his spiritual eye sight, his spiritual ears, and change his circumstances by speaking words of faith, etc. I stayed amazed as he asked me questions in humility and started wanting to please me in ways that he had never done before. What an amazing God we serve!

I prayed for my children, calling them the smartest kids in the world. I also prayed for myself; confessing the Word: *I am dead to sin but alive in God* (Romans 6:11)*; I will study the Word of God; I will pray* (II Timothy 2:15; Luke 18:1)*; I take every thought captive unto the obedience of Jesus Christ, casting down every imagination, and every high and lofty thing that exalt itself against the knowledge of God* (II Corinthians 10:5)*; No weapon formed against me shall prosper, but every tongue that rise against me in judgment, I shall show to be wrong* (Isaiah 54:17)*; I do not think more highly of myself than I ought to in the flesh* (Romans 12:3) *I am purposed that my mouth shall not transgress. I will speak forth the righteousness and praise of God all the day long* (Psalm 17:3; 35:28)*; God has not given me the spirit of fear, but one of power, love, and a sound mind* (II Timothy 1:7).

Conquer the Spirit of Offense

"And then many will be offended and repelled and will begin to distrust and desert [Him Whom they ought to trust and obey] and will stumble and fall away, and betray one another and pursue one another with hatred." Matthew 24:10

Our level of maturity will determine how well we handle stress and offense. We have all had our feelings hurt at some time in our lives. We've heard unkind remarks about us or had someone say something unkind right to our face. Some of us have even been abused verbally, mentally or physically. Some of us may have felt violated at some point, and have never been able to forget the pain that was felt. When feelings are hurt, it opens the door for a spirit of offense to come in.

On the other hand, we need to be cautious that some of our own actions can cause others to become offended; we may unwittingly provoke some negative actions; and if so, change those actions. We should not do those things that we know are offensive and insulting to others. Be aware of what we think and before we speak. Our words can destroy a person's self-esteem or they can bring them up to a higher level. The closer you are to a person, the more hurtful an offense can be. Satan knows that.

If you've been hurt and not healed, it is almost inevitable that you will carry those hurts into relationships and end up wounding others. This is true because we can only give that which we have to give. If all you have are open wounds, then it is certain that you will open wounds. It is extremely difficult to have healthy relationships when you continue to carry around all the hurts from your past. The Word of God can change that.

Psalm 119:16 says *"Great peace have they who love Your law. Nothing shall offend them or make them stumble."* You may want to write that scripture in the back of your bible and look at it from time to time. Begin confessing *"I love God's Word above my feelings. I love God's Word above making myself feel satisfied at holding a grudge against someone who has hurt me. I love God's Word and because I love His law, I am going to have great peace in my life. I am not going to stumble."*

"The entrance and unfolding of Your Words give light; their unfolding give understanding (discernment and comprehension) to the simple." Psalm 119:130

The entrance of God's Word brings light, which is something we all need. We do not always know or see what we need to do; and many times we do not recognize our own problems. We need God's light to understand ourselves and to see how we need to change and how we can cooperate with God to make things better. Reading God's Word is like looking in a mirror. It enables us to see what needs to be cleaned up in our lives. Either you will conquer the Spirit of Offense in your life or it will conquer you.

Guard Your Third Ear

"She speaks with wisdom, and faithful instruction is on her tongue." Proverbs 31:26

Be careful who you choose to reveal your personal issues to. Much caution should also be given to the mentors a woman chooses to listen to concerning her relationships—before and during marriage. The mentor with a *regenerate* heart will speak of love and the need to commit the relationship to God. The mentor with an *unregenerate* heart will speak only of failure, distrust and a need to "honey, don't let that man tell you what to do! You keep your independence!"

That kind of advice will soon have you sleeping alone and going from relationship to relationship looking for joy and happiness in someone who is incapable of making you content and happy. You see, joy and happiness comes only from God. (Psalm 16:11) It is not your spouse's job to give you these things. In fact, these qualities should be already present in you as a drawing card to a potential companion. Worship and relationship with God gives you the gift of joy and happiness as a spiritual outpouring to obedience in relationship lines up more and more with the Word of God.

Finding an older, wiser couple who has endured and weathered the storm may be a good place to start. However, caution is needed in this area since couples may remain together for all sorts of reasons that have nothing to do with love. The measuring stick for seeking godly advice is to look at the fruit being produced in a possible mentor's life— longevity in relationship, peace and harmony, etc... If a possible mentor is not happy in relationship, then they may only be able to give you advice that may lead you to the same unhappy conclusion in relationship. Of course, a mentor who has lost a spouse through death, sickness, or unwanted divorce, etc., cannot be blamed for lack of longevity. The point is the Holy Spirit dwelling in another will never contradict the Word of God. God's Word speaks of love covering a multitude of sins, endurance and peace; He will not speak through another to encourage division, war and hatred.

Keep the Faith

"For in the gospel the righteousness of God is revealed--a righteousness that is by faith from first to last, just as it is written: "The righteous will live by faith."
Romans 1:17

I am reminded here of the night I ran out of gas on Interstate 95 going North. I was quite a distance from the next exit and it was pitch dark outside. Even though I was in a new car, I failed to notice when the gas light went off because I was too into the gospel music I was listening to. Suddenly, my car sputtered and began to slow down. The gas pedal no longer had an effect. "OMG!!!" "I am out of gas." I pondered what to do. Finally, I used my cell phone to give my location to the Highway Patrol. After that, there was nothing left to do but wait. And wait I did, for over two solid hours - casting down imaginations about what might be lurking in the woods; scooting down and covering my head with passing cars. At one point, I thought "Nobody will wonder where I am or care when I get home because I live alone." But I quickly brightened. God will care. Just like the song I had listened to, "His eye is on the Sparrow, and I know He watches me." I prayed no one would stop to help because I felt too vulnerable to trust.

"Stand still, and see the salvation of the Lord." Exodus 14:13

These words contain God's command to the believer when she is reduced to great strains and brought into extraordinary difficulties. She cannot retreat; she cannot go forward; she is shut upon the right hand and on the left. What is she now to do?

The Master's word to her is "stand still." It will be well for her if, at such times, she listens only to her Master's word, for other and evil advisers come with their own suggestions. Despair whispers, "Lie down and die; give it all up!" But God would have us put on a cheerful courage, and even in our worst times, rejoice in His love and faithfulness

Cowardice says, "Retreat; go back to the worldly way of acting; you cannot play the Christian's part; it is too difficult for you. Relinquish God's principles."

But, however much Satan may urge this course upon you; you cannot follow it, if you are a child of God. His divine fiat has bid thee go from strength to strength, and so thou shalt, and neither death nor hell shall turn thee from thy course. What if for a while you are called to stand still; yet this is but to renew your strength for some greater advance in due time.

Precipitancy cries, "Do something; stir yourself; to stand still and wait is sheer idleness." We must be doing something at once – we must do it, so we think – instead of looking to the LORD, who will not only do something, but will do everything.

Presumption boasts, "If the sea be before you, march into it, and expect a miracle." But faith listens neither to presumption, nor to despair, nor to cowardice nor to precipitancy, but it hears God say, "Stand still," and immovable as a rock it stands

"Stand still" – keep the posture of an upright man, ready for action, expecting further orders, cheerfully and patiently awaiting His directing voice; and it will not be long before God shall say to you, as distinctly as Moses said it to the people of Israel, "Go forward!"

Listen!!!

"... whatever Sarah tells you, **listen** to **her** ... Genesis 21:12

"After the earthquake came a fire, but the LORD was not in the fire. And after the fire came a gentle whisper." 1 Kings 19:12

It's important to be a good listener. God often speaks to us through others. I dare say fifty percent of arguments can be solved if we would but be certain of what the speaker is truly saying to us.

By learning to **listen effectively**, we can set up an atmosphere of trust. Listening effectively means to be alert, sitting up straight and leaning slightly forward - if appropriate distance can be maintained without becoming distracting. Let your face radiate interest in the speaker's story. Everyone feels their story is important and everyone has a story to be told. Know when it is critical not to interject your opinion or comments. Smile only when it is appropriate to show you understand. Ask questions when you need clarification.

React to ideas and not to the person. Do not allow your reaction to the person to influence your interpretation of the speaker's words. Good ideas can come even from persons you don't like.

When you are listening, **do not argue a point mentally** to keep from setting up a listening barrier. Do not be concerned with planning a response. Be alert to changes in facial expressions, gestures, body positions. Body language is more revealing than actual words. When you spot a furrowed brow or clenched fist, you need to listen with your eyes as well as your ears. The situation may be going from oral to physical.

Concentrate on voice tone. Like gestures, they can indicate the emotional meanings behind words. For instance, the same sentence can indicate many different meanings depending on the way the words are emphasized or the tone in which they are spoken.

Listen for what the speaker is trying to accomplish by his remarks. Be sensitive to different levels of meaning in what the person tells you, and be prepared to decipher those levels. People often expect you to read their minds through innuendos or hints. For instance, what if your love interest says, "I suppose I should stay home on Saturday and paint the bedroom," and then waits for your response. Does he want you to talk him out of it? Does he want your encouragement? Or does he want your help? You have to learn to read the other...

Try to detach from your emotions – your worries, enthusiasm, anger, fear, etc. These emotions will distract you from listening well and may cause you to jump to the wrong conclusions.

Get rid of distractions. Good listening will be enhanced if you choose the proper time and situation to bring up a conversation. A person watching a sports program on television is less likely to be willing or able to listen attentively to anything else at the moment. Another important distraction is having someone else around. The intended listener may feel they have to save face (cover their true feelings).

Never begin a conversation with "so and so said," The intended listener may react to so and so and not the issue at hand; they may feel you have already embraced an accusation. Better to feel out the person, for instance "I heard that Jane's husband falsely accused her of being unfaithful, you would never accuse me before hearing my side of a piece of gossip, would you?" Another good response is, "With all due respect, I am concerned about something. May I discuss it with you now?" Here are some others.

Stop Talking. You cannot listen while you are talking. A godly hint is to look at the anatomy of your own head. You have two ears and one mouth; therefore, do twice as much listening. Saying nothing is a very good way to communicate genuine acceptance of the importance of what the speaker is saying. An alternative to saying nothing is to making such comments as "You really mean that don't you?" Or "I didn't know you felt this way," or simply "huh-huh," at appropriate intervals. Or how about "Let me think about that?"

Love Above All Else

In Matthew 22:35-40, the Jews were not finished questioning Jesus. A lawyer asked, "Which commandment is the greatest of all?" Jesus answered expounding from the Old Testament:

"Love the Lord your God with all your heart, and with all your soul,
and with all your mind and with all your strength."

He added a second command that *we must love our neighbor as ourselves.* Then he explained that every other law of God was based on these two laws.

Let's explore what Jesus may have meant when He said we are to love God with all our heart, soul, mind and strength? God's kind of love is called Agape. It is different from the world's kind of love. God's meaning of *Love* is putting others first. Loving others – not judging - is a reflection of God's love in us and for us.

> *"But God demonstrates his own love for us in this:*
> *While we were still sinners, Christ died for us."* Romans 5:8

Sacrifice is giving up something, or doing without in order to meet the greater need of others. If our spouse has not yet accepted salvation, they do not have the Holy Spirit to fight temptation. We need to pray for them.

> *"The natural person does not accept the things of the Spirit of God,*
> *for they are folly to him, and he is not able to understand them*
> *because they are spiritually discerned."* 1 Corinthians 2:14

Devotion is being committed to God and His plans for our life. Not wanting to have our own way all the time. Commitment to our marriage covenant means understanding that the covenant is greater than our own selfish desires. Our children and extended family members are learning from what we say and do. There are long range effects to our yet unborn grands that we cannot fathom.

Likewise, our *heart* is the seat of our emotions and affections; while our *soul* is our *conscience and* what makes us alive. Our *mind* is our brain, the part that thinks things through. Our *strength* is our will, our desire and our commitment. Our Spirit is that part that is able to connect, worship and commune with God.

In this passage of Scripture, I believe Jesus means all the things that make up the whole self must be devoted to God. It's not enough for our heart to love God but our *Will* to be too lazy and want to do nothing. Nor can our *soul* believe in God but our *mind* has doubts.

Note that love is not just a feeling. If so, the feeling would change according to circumstances; but true love is steady.

"Whatever is good and perfect comes down to us from God our Father,
who created all the lights in the heavens. He never changes or casts
a shifting shadow." James 1:17

It tries to understand rather than react irrationally. It is both *total* and *sacrificial*. However, there are few people in life who are totally committed to anything.

An illustration of total commitment may be seen in comparing the training of Olympic athletes who are totally committed to their sport. Every decision they make hinges on whether it will help or hurt their goal of becoming an excellent athlete. What they eat, how often they practice, where they go, and who they spend time with is all determined by whether it helps them meet or whether it hinders reaching their goal.

Even the apostle Paul used Olympic athletes as examples of how Christians should live their lives.

"Do you not know that in a race all the runners run, but only one gets the prize? Run in
such a way as to get the prize. Everyone who competes in the games goes into strict
training. They do it to get a crown that will not last; but we [Christians] do it to get a
crown that will last forever." 1 Corinthians 9:24-25

Accordingly, if you love God, you will not ignore Him or speak badly about Him. If you love your neighbor, you will not steal from them or hurt them. All the other laws (don't covet, don't take the Lord's name in vain, etc.) are based on loving God or loving man.

This understanding should dramatically affect and change our lifestyle as we realize that we cannot love God and be unfaithful. We must only love Him. Then He will give us that perfect love for our spouses and our family and our fellow man.

But we cannot love God and do nothing.

Now someone may argue, "Some people have faith; others have good deeds." But I
say, "How can you show me your faith if you don't have good deeds? I will show
you my faith by my good deeds." James 2:18

Loving someone means doing things for them, caring about them and their feelings; and it means giving up our time, and money and things for them.

142

"By their fruits you will easily recognize them. Are grapes gathered from thorns or figs from brambles?" Matthew 7:16

In other words, persons may claim to love, that is the inward appearance. What they do with that love reveals whether the Holy Spirit is working within. If there is contradiction between what they say and what they do, there is no truth in their profession of love because their outward fruit reveals who they really are.

Move in Divine Forgiveness

"But if you do not forgive, neither will your Father who is in heaven forgive your transgressions." Mark 11:26

If our goal is to have successful relationships, we must first know who we are in Christ. Through salvation, we gain access to all God has to offer, including spiritual discernment. Right after beginning His ministry, Jesus was taken into the wilderness to be tested. You also will be tested. The Word of God will be your roadmap as you navigate through this life. God wishes us to be wise as to what is good, and simple-minded as to what is evil. Therefore, watch your focus.

Spiritual discernment is the grace to see into the unseen. It is a gift of the Holy Spirit to perceive what is in the spirit. The purpose of the gift is to see into the nature of that which is veiled. To see what is controlling each person we encounter. But the first veil that must be removed is the veil over our own hearts; so that in the process, we discover the depravity and selfishness of our own carnal nature. Jesus demands we understand our own need of His mercy so that, out of the grace we have received, we can then compassionately minister to others. In other words, you are not fit to minister to others until you fully understand the mercy that has been given to you. Only then will we know thoroughly that the gift of discernment is not a faculty of our own minds.

We must ever be conscious that Christ's goal is to save, not to judge. We are called to navigate the narrow and well-hidden path of life into the true nature of human need. If we are truly to help, not hurt, we must remember we are following a Lamb. This foundation must be laid correctly, for if you have discernment, you cannot react. To perceive, you must make yourself blind to what seems apparent. People may react to you, but you must always remain forgiving in nature, for the demons you cast out may speak to you in the person's voice, masquerading as the individual himself. Remember, we wrestle not against flesh and blood.

For this very reason, Jesus said, *"Whoever shall speak a word against the Son of Man, it shall be forgiven him"* (Matthew 12:32). Jesus prepared His heart to forgive men before they ever sinned against Him. He knew His mission was to die for men, not to condemn them. Take time now to ask yourself, what your mission is. If it is to have an abundant life and live in harmony with everyone, then you must use the rules set up by God to do so. You must be willing to die to self-defense; to the ways of the world and listen to the voice of the Holy Spirit and Godly mentors in your life.

In all areas of life, we are not only called into Christ's life, but into His mission as well. Jesus said, "As Thou didst send Me into the world, I also have sent them." (1 John 17:18). To join ourselves in marriage to another is to be called to die to our own fleshly desires so that our spouse (and family) may live. That is why it is critical to choose a Godly companion or a teachable one. Before our perception develops, our love must develop until our normal attitude is one of perpetual forgiveness. Love is the strongest warfare tool we have. God is love, and love never fails. Love will bind the enemy and break bonds to set the captives free.

If God will show us the hearts of men and use us to release them from captivity, we cannot react to what they ***say***. As our perception becomes more like that of Christ Himself, we cannot even react to what they ***do.*** We can only listen and be prepared to make decisions that will affect ***our own lives.***

If we do not move in divine forgiveness, we will walk in much deception. We will presume we have discernment when, in truth, we are seeing through the veil of a "critical spirit." We must know our weaknesses, for if we are blind to our sins, what we assume we discern in men will merely be the reflection of ourselves. Indeed, if we do not move in love, we will actually become a menace to the body of Christ rather than a blessing.

Possess the Land

"This book of the law shall not depart out of thy mouth; but thou shalt meditate therein day and night, that thou may observe to do according to all that is written therein: for then thou shalt make thou way prosperous, and then thou shall have good success." Joshua 1:8

God's Word is the way He speaks to us all His promises and His blessings. But we live in a natural world that contradicts God's Word and constantly shows us tragedy, pain and suffering. Some things have become so real until we forget that God is Spirit and lives in the world of the unseen. We rub shoulders with the physical day after day until the unseen realm of the spirit seems unreal. We are almost tempted to believe it doesn't exist. But Paul said:

"For our light affliction, which is but a moment, worketh for us a far more exceeding and eternal weight of glory; While we look not at the things which are seen, but at the things which are not seen; for the things which are seen are temporal; but the things which are not seen are eternal." 2 Corinthians 4:17, 18

These words almost cause us to think the Apostle Paul had lost his mind when he said; **Look not at the things which are seen.** How in the world can you look at something that you can't see!

Paul is talking about unseen principles: principles that make God's Word work for you, which are actually spiritual laws.

The word law is defined as "the body of rules and principles governing the affairs of a community and enforced by a legal system."

The laws of God are simply the ways in which He works. The spirit realm works according to God's system of laws and affects everything in the world. An example of one of His laws is the law of sowing and reaping. In this law we find that whatever you sow – money, time, physical possessions, prayer, etc. – you will reap. Whatever you give, you will receive in like kind. The law of sowing and reaping is a spiritual law that affects you, regardless of whether or not you believe it or not.

There are many other examples of different laws throughout the Bible. Genesis 8:22 says, "While the earth remains, seedtime and harvest, and cold and heat, and summer and winter, and day and night shall not cease."

In addition to spiritual laws, we are also governed by natural laws. They are called "natural" because they govern the natural world and they work in the same way spiritual laws work. For example, the law of gravity does not ask for your permission or approval to work. It automatically works whether you want it to or not. It is a natural law you live with every day.

Spiritual laws or forces are unseen; and supersede or override physical laws. Spiritual forces are eternal forces which always work when the righteous set them in motion.

Notice when the Apostle Paul said, *"For our light affliction, which is but a moment, worketh for us a far more exceeding and eternal weight of glory; While we look not at the things which are seen …*

The focal word is "while." In other words, if you're looking at seen things [problems, challenges, sufferings, etc.], things of the natural, then these afflictions will not work an exceeding weight of glory for you. God would not tell us in Matthew 6 not to worry if it were not possible to do so. It will work only while you are looking at things which are not seen. The Fruit of the Spirit ate things which cannot be seen with the natural eye [love, peace, joy, longsuffering. Etc.]

You must shift over into the realm of spiritual law and begin to look at things which are not seen with the natural eye.

> *"Now faith is the substance of things hoped for; the evidence of*
> *things not seen."* Hebrews 11:1

You look at things which are not seen with the eye of the spirit – the eye of faith. Examples would be when I called my husband a man of God consistently while he was still running around in the streets. He just didn't know it yet [see "Women are Spiritual BRIDGES," p. 294). I also called my children the smarted kids that ever lived. I am sure many who saw in the natural what was happening with my husband and kids thought I was lying or simply out of my mind. But because I was following God's Word and speaking in faith, I was shaping the unseen. I am slowly seeing all that I spoke come to past. Though no longer among the living, I saw my husband confess Jesus as his Lord before he passed away.

Don't look at the way things are [lack] but at how they are going to be [the substance of things hoped for which is called faith].

Paul said that pressure will work for you an exceeding eternal weight of glory *if you will look at things which are not seen.* It is actually "the looking at the unseen" that brings the glory, not the pressure of the affliction.

This agrees with what he said in Philippians 4:8: *"Finally, brethren, whatsoever things are honest, whatsoever things are just, whatsoever things are pure, whatsoever things are lovely, whatsoever things are of good report; if there be any praise, think on these things."*

In other words, get your mind off the problem and begin to think on the things you desire, the things you don't see with your physical eye. When you learn to see the answer by the *Eye of Faith*, then you will possess the Land – make your way prosperous by possessing wisdom and all the promises that God made to Abraham and His descendants – God's chosen people.

Recognize You have an Enemy

Satan is an equal opportunity persecutor. Bren Gandy-Wilson

You must recognize you have an enemy; do not become an unwitting accomplice to Satan's evil schemes. Recognize he is persecuting your loved ones and neighbor as yourself. First Peter five and eight tells us to "Be well balanced (temperate, sober of mind), be vigilant and cautious at all times; for that enemy of yours, the devil, roams around like a lion [roaring in fierce hunger], seeking someone to seize upon and devour. *(Amplified Bible)* To be sober means to avoid drunkenness of your senses, and drunkenness in your souls; be not overcharged with the concerns of this world. To be vigilant means to keep awake; be always watchful; never be off your guard because your enemies are alert, they are never off theirs.

The adversary in this verse is referred to as *"your"* adversary. You must recognize the enemy behind people's actions. That's why Jesus said pray for your enemies. They are unaware of how Satan is using them. Many homes are destroyed because of lack of understanding. Pray that their eyes be opened to who their real enemy is.

Sad to say but most Christians do not believe they have an adversary. Neither do they realize that the adversary referred to in this verse is people who intentionally serve the will of Satan. If you do not believe you have an enemy, then you have no reason to remain alert and watchful to provocations. Put on God's whole armor [the armor of a heavy-armed soldier which God supplies], that you may be able successfully to stand up against [all] the strategies *and* the deceits of the devil.

In Ephesians 6, Paul tells us "that we are not wrestling with flesh and blood [contending only with physical opponents], but against the despotisms, against the powers, against [the master spirits who are] the world rulers of this present darkness, against the spirit forces of wickedness in the heavenly (supernatural) sphere.

Therefore put on God's complete armor, that you may be able to resist *and* stand your ground on the evil day [of danger], and, having done all [the crisis demands], to stand [firmly in your place]. Stand therefore [hold your ground], having tightened the belt of truth around your loins and having put on the breastplate of integrity *and* of moral rectitude *and* right standing with God, And having shod your feet in preparation [to face the enemy with the firm-footed stability, the promptness, and the readiness produced by the good news] of the Gospel of peace.

Lift up over all the [covering] shield of saving faith, upon which you can quench all the flaming missiles of the wicked [one]. And take the helmet of salvation and the sword that the Spirit wields, which is the Word of God. Pray at all times (on every occasion, in every season) in the Spirit, with all [manner of] prayer and entreaty. To that end keep alert and watch with strong purpose *and* perseverance, interceding in behalf of all the saints (God's consecrated people)."

While you are meddling in everybody else's business and wondering why so-and-so is so foolish in her decision-making, Satan is watching you. While you are judging and have no understanding of why that woman is allowing that no good man to control her life, Satan has one lined up for you.

He will study your comments and your personality, and then fashion someone just for you—and wait to send him into your life at just the right time—if you are not watchful. Being watchful means standing on the bank and observing what is being drawn towards you. Is he willing to serve God or the devil?

Women are warned in First Peter five and eight to be sober and vigilant because they have an ever active, implacable, subtle enemy to contend with. He walks about - he has access to you everywhere; he knows your feelings and your propensities, and informs himself of all your circumstances; only God can know more and do more than he, therefore all your care **must** be cast upon Him for He cares for you and has a good life planned for you. (Jeremiah 29:11)

But don't forget that your love one is also in this same battle. Satan is an equal opportunity persecutor. Jesus knew this. That's why He could look down from the cross and say "Father forgive them for they know not what they do" (Luke 23:34). Jesus understood that the people were being controlled by the same evil influence that convinced Eve to eat of the forbidden fruit. You must become a nonconformist! Don't become a hater. Decide to pray for both your family, friends and even your enemies. Understand they need your prayers even though they may not want them. Nobody can keep you from praying or fasting or singing God's praises.

Temptation

*"in order that Satan might not outwit us. For we are not
unaware of his schemes."* 2Corinthians 2:11

Satan tempts under three forms: 1) the subtle serpent; to beguile your senses through promising much, but giving very little; through perverting your judgment by confusing the issues of life and enchanting your imagination. 2) as an angel of light to deceive with many kindnesses; to deceive us with false views of spiritual things, refinements in religion, and presumption on the providence and grace of God; and 3) as a roaring lion; to bear us down, and destroy us by violent opposition, persecution, and death. Later in Chapter IX: *Relationship Dynamics*, we will see how these three forms play out in relationships.

He walks about, traversing the earth, seeking whom he may devour - Whom he may gulp down. It is not every one that he can swallow down. He cannot swallow down those who are sober and vigilant. Sobriety and vigilance comes from studying and applying God's Word. These persons are proof against Satan. However, those who are fretting with the cares of this world, "I am incomplete without a man in my life" - and are not watchful, these he may swallow down. Be careful, this great need will show up not only in how you dress and carry yourself, but also in every decision you make in life.

It is hard enough to navigate through this world; making wise decisions, without complicating the matter by fogging up your brain with addictive chemicals. This verse admonishes us to be sober, do not drink and do not swallow down. If you swallow strong drink down, the devil will swallow you down. But strong drink is not the devil's only way to you, he may use any vice or fleshly (unscriptural) desire to gain a foothold into your life – if you are not discerning.

"The house of the wicked will be destroyed, But the tent of the upright will flourish.
There is a way which seems right to a man, But its end is the way of death.
Even in laughter the heart may be in pain, And the end of joy may be grief...." Proverbs 14:11-13

Do not be tempted to go out and cheat in an established relationship. If you cannot handle one relationship, how are you going to handle two? If you do, you will move outside of the protection of God. You will move into Satan's territory – stripped of the armor of God, you are ill equipped to do battle against all that Satan has in store for you: the spirit of addiction, venereal diseases, mental illnesses, un-forgiveness, bitterness, bad health, unethical habits and unspiritual habits, etc.

Do not be in too big of a hurry to rebound from a destructive relationship. Sit a while. Meditate on what went wrong before. Acknowledge your part in it. It is never one hundred percent the other person's fault. Ask God for His help in your next steps.

Shut Your Mouth!

"All their days their work is grief and pain; even at night their minds do not rest. This too is meaningless." Ecclesiastes 2:23

"Cease striving and know that I am God; I will be exalted among the nations, I will be exalted in the earth. The LORD of hosts is with us; The God of Jacob is our stronghold. Selah." Psalm 46:20

Perhaps "Be Quiet," or "Hush," might be a more appropriate term to use in order to keep from offending. However, I wanted to get your attention. Sometimes if you are going to exchange the seen for the unseen (what you see for what you desire), you have to shut your mouth! No one can repeat unspoken words or gossip about silent thoughts. When God is working in your life, He may reveal hope on the way. You have to keep God's secrets to prevent the enemy from trying to block what God is sending your way.

"...in which you used to live when you followed the ways of this world and of the ruler of the kingdom of the air, the spirit who is now at work in those who are disobedient." Ephesians 2:2

Take Zachariah, for instance. God sent the Angel Gabriel to speak to him. Gabriel said, "Fear not Zacharias, for your prayer is heard; and your wife Elizabeth shall bear you a son, and you shall call his name John. [Luke 1:13]

Zachariah and Elizabeth had been praying for this. But when God sent the angel with the message that their prayers were going to be answered, Zachariah said, "How do I know you're telling the truth? Give me a sign." [verse 18, paraphrased]

Gabriel probably thought, "If we don't get his mouth shut, he is going to use it to speak doubts into existence that will interfere with God's plan." God pressed the angel to shut Zacharias' mouth shut!

Gabriel said, "All right I'm going to give you a sign. By this sign you will know that all that I have said will come to pass. [Not only that, he was insuring that it would come to pass!] You will be dumb and not able to speak until it happens."

Here you see the wisdom of God. God said "I'll take the things that are not and bring to naught the things that are." Words that are not spoken are much more powerful than words that are spoken in unbelief.

When God reveals things to you through revelation, Scripture or circumstances, He doesn't intend for you to tell everybody. You must keep God's secrets. Otherwise, those you speak to may speak words of doubt and try to convince you to doubt God's unseen promises.

I've seen some things in my spirit that I have kept to myself so the devil doesn't know about it When I pray, I pray in the spirit. The devil sure would like to know what it is so he can try to head it off. He doesn't know and I'm not going to tell him, even though I could unwittingly through my prayers.

Sometimes you can unwittingly give the devil valuable information when you pray. Let me give an example: A man is attacked by two robbers while he is walking down the street. A gun is stuck in his ribs, "Give us your money, they demand. Because he is a man of faith, he drops to his knees to pray. Prayer is good for everything right? The man throws his hands up into the air and says, "Oh God, please don't let them find that one-hundred dollar bill I put in my sock!"

Likewise, if you go around telling your business, even to well meaning Christians, they may speak words of doubt and get spiritual things all out of shape. Sometimes silence is more important than prayer – or rehashing unfortunate circumstances.

Hear me now! Many spouses have been offended because someone asks them about troubling circumstances they had not revealed. Others have been wooed away from their marriages because their better half sought comfort from someone who decided, "Oh Oh! There's trouble in Paradise!" This individual decided to use the words of the complaining spouse to formulate a plan of action to gain the affections of their spouse.

Ten Guidelines For Detecting Abusers

"I applied my mind to study and to explore by wisdom all that is done under the heavens. What a heavy burden God has laid on mankind!" Ecclesiastes 1:13

Just as there are no assurances in life, there is no claim in this book that by following certain steps you will be guaranteed a trouble-free relationship. But there is the claim of God's help if you are obedient to *"Trust in the LORD with all of your heart and lean not to your own understanding. In all of your ways, acknowledge Him and He will strengthen your heart."* (Psalm 3:4-5)

There are countless attachments that we form in the world. Another name for attachment is commitment. Every attachment brings with it burdens and responsibilities to be discerning. Let me illustrate. If you buy a car, you are attaching yourself to all that the car demands for it to remain useful. There is insurance, gas, registration, maintenance, taxes, etc., continuously. Therefore, preplanning and understanding the coming obligations ahead of time is very necessary to following through and avoiding repossession.

God-ordained attachments will put you in a position to ask God for what you need or want and confidently expect that He will answer you (John 15:7). On the other hand, wrong attachments can place demands on you, draining you of your strength and resources, and pull you off God's plan and timing for His best to manifest in your life.

Here are 10 Steps to help you recognize your lifetime companion during the dating phase:

Step 1: **Be honest with anyone you date**. No hedging around about what it is you are looking for. If your goal is to get married, do not allow a love interest to believe you might settle for less (in hopes of luring them in later). This could lead to feelings of anger, entrapment and a sense of feeling deceived that cannot be overcome. By being honest, insincere dates will weed themselves out.

Step 2: Stay focused. Do not complicate the relationship with premarital sex. It will be difficult enough getting to know the heart of your love interest and they you, without adding the risk of "spirit deposits" through sexual intercourse (Remember, this is how a marriage is consummated).

Men are natural hunters (dominion gone wild after the fall). Most men will believe a woman they can conquer before marriage unworthy of becoming their lifetime companion.

Even if you are overcome with compassion because you are absolutely sure "this is the one," men don't think the same way women think. A man will not think it flattering to their powers of persuasion, but think of you as weak and susceptible to being tempted by other men when the occasion arises.

Step 3: Read and Apply the Word of God for strength and discernment. Be absolutely familiar with all God has to say about marriage, family and how to treat others. Read other godly books and manuals on the marriage relationship. This will be a light unto your path, pointing you in the right direction, helping you rightly divide the Word, and steering you away from dates who don't share God's point of view in these areas.

Step 4: Stay close to godly mentors. Consult them often concerning how the relationship is progressing. Do not trust only your own judgment when issues or pressures arise. You may under react or over react during emotional distress or elation without proper and objective advice.

Step 5: **Pray**. Make a list of the godly qualities you would like in a lifetime companion. Present these to God and ask for His discernment. Remember that prayer is a two-way conversation. Stay open to God's promptings and revelations. Biblical prayers are marked by humility and honesty before God. They are wide-ranging and specific. As Solomon led the people in prayer, he asked God to hear their prayers concerning a variety of situations: 1) crime (6:22-23); 2) enemy attacks (6:24-25); 3) drought (6:26-27); 4) famine (6:28-31); 5) influx of foreigners (6:32-33); 6) war (6:34-35; 7) sin (6:36-39). God is concerned with whatever we are facing; even the difficult consequences we bring upon ourselves. He wants us to turn to Him in prayer—not just to other people. When you pray, remember that God hears every word you say; Jesus sighs with you. Don't give room to the devil by letting the extremity of your situation cause you to doubt God's care for you.

Step 6: **Fast.** You and your love interest should fast as well as pray for one another for discernment as well as for repentance. *"But when you fast, comb your hair and wash your face. Then no one will suspect you are fasting, except your Father, who knows what you do in secret. "And your Father, who knows all secrets, will reward."* (Matthew 6:17-18)

Fasting together or separately needs to be done for the right reason. Fasting (or going without food in order to spend time in prayer), is noble but difficult. Fasting even for short periods gives time to pray, teaches self-discipline, reminds that you can live with a lot less and helps you appreciate God's gifts.

In Matthew six, Jesus was not condemning fasting, but hypocrisy—fasting in order to gain public approval. Fasting was mandatory for the Jewish people once a year, on the Day of Atonement (Leviticus 23:32). The Pharisees voluntarily fasted twice a week to impress the people with their "holiness." Jesus commended acts of self-sacrifice done quietly and sincerely. He wanted people to adopt spiritual disciplines for the right reasons not for a selfish desire for praise.

> *"He prayed, 'O LORD, God of Israel, there is no God like you in all of heaven and earth. You keep your promises and show unfailing love to all who obey you and are eager to do your will."* (2 Chronicles 6:14)

Step 7: Have Patience. Do not jump to conclusions or make rash decisions each time you meet someone. Satan is real and will send counterfeits your way. Be prepared to follow the leading of the Holy Spirit. Remember, a "No" in this relationship may mean a "Yes" to a relationship in the future. In this matter, time will be your best ally. Why? Because over time it is hard to keep up an act. You will eventually know if your love interest is reacting to you in the opposite way that a God-fearing person should. If so, you should conclude that, they have no regard for the Word of God or His laws. God is Love. If they have not learned to love God, they will be unable to love themselves or to love you.

Step 8: Pay attention to conversation, expression and environments. "Out of the heart the mouth speaks." The tongue is the safest way to gauge a person's true feelings. Even the most accomplished con will reveal their true feelings over time – once they feel comfortable in the relationship.

Step 9: Pay attention to patterns. The "Law of Repetition" has been activated in this relationship when your love interest uses your actions and words as examples of why they left a previous relationship. They will continue to compare you to the love that went wrong until you get the message. A red flag should also go up for you if you witness too many similar incidences to a past relationship that went sour. Whatever needed to be learned in the previous relationship was not learned and will continue to be repeated until you or they learn to make different choices and decisions.

Step 10: **Spend Time in God's Presence**. *"Now faith is the substance of things hoped for, the evidence of things not seen."* (Hebrews 11:1). Spending time in praise and worship, fasting and praying together strengthens faith and confidence so that the parties involved will believe that all things are possible by believing in the power of God. By spending time in God's presence, couples grow closer and believe in God's power to help them through difficult times and to bless and prosper them and their children. Your love one should be someone who is captivated by what captivates you and grows spiritually with you; one who attends worship, pursues a knowledge of God without your urging and is comfortable in the presence of worthy mentors.

If you feel you cannot trust the one you wish to marry to pursue knowledge of God without your constant encouragement, this is a deal breaker. This means they truly do not desire to know God. Even if a person is exciting, articulate, vibrant and lovable, if they only attend church to please you, or avoid your nagging or begging, any hope of a happy marriage, without the authority of God in your intended lifetime companion's life, is a mere fantasy.

Definitely run for the hills if you feel the one you wish to marry has not been captivated by what has captivated you. You might as well because you are doomed to spend a lot of quality time alone. If the Holy Spirit and the things of God have captivated you: attending church, Bible Study, Sunday school, etc. You delight in reading the Bible daily or sitting around discussing the things of God, and these things have not captivated them. In fact, they are more captivated by play and foreplay than the Presence of the Holy Spirit in the Secret Place; therefore, the same things that stir you have not stirred them. You cannot know a person by studying them. You know a person by studying their focus. The strongest people I know are ones who know how to stand on their knees before God; to cry at the mention of the gospel, and to receive criticism graciously.

There is no hope of greatness ever being birth in this individual if your love one is uncomfortable in the presence of God. All success comes from God. You can date a person who is attractive, refined, and intelligent and hovers at your feet, but if they hate the presence of God, that person will never be more than what you see today. Every preacher will become their rival. They will become intimidated by your choice to attend church. When you come home late from a Wednesday night Bible service, they will accuse you of having someone else on the side. Unsaved people are often intimidated by believing people because they know in their hearts that a person who walks with God has something they lack.

An accident is just waiting to happen if you feel your love one does not hunger to know the voice of God. Obedience is the secret of every successful person. The Bible is God's

Voice. If a man or woman disdains the Voice of Truth and Wisdom - they will birth a parade of tragedies and catastrophes throughout their life. Their very decisions will create losses. Their weaknesses will flourish. Unlawful desires will rage like an inferno. Such a relationship is an invitation to commit spiritual suicide.

Use Spiritual Weapons to Fight

"The weapons we fight with are not the weapons of the world. On the contrary,
they have divine power to demolish strongholds." 2 Corinthians 10:6

The story of a man walking with a coat on in the desert represents a closed heart hiding in the shadows; trying to survive. The sun and wind decided to have a contest to see which of them could cause him to remove his coat. The wind went first. The wind represents harshness. The wind that comes out of our mouth to chastise others may be all lightning and thunder, but provide no rain of refreshing understanding and love to open the heart and draw out repentance. The wind blew as hard as it could upon the man walking but could not make him remove his coat. Instead, he pulled it even tighter around about himself.

Then the sun decided to try. The sun represents a steady gentleness that will not be shaken. It begins to beat down warm rays of love, mercy and grace upon the man. The man begins to remember his body and care that it was being overheated in its present environment. So he removed his coat.

When we come into a marriage relationship, we affect the lives of our mate for the good or for the worse. We, like our mate, are merely weak humans, but we don't need to use human plans and methods to win our battles. Differences can provide opportunities to practice what we read in the Bible.

When dealing with the pride that keeps people from a relationship with Christ and from each other, we may be tempted to use our own methods. But nothing can break down these barriers like God's weapons of truth and righteousness.

God's mighty weapons, the weapons by which we hope to live a victorious life, are available to us as we fight against Satan's strongholds. The word rendered here as "strongholds" mean properly a fastness, fortress, or strong fortification. It is here beautifully used to denote the various obstacles resembling a fortress which exist, and which are designed and adapted to oppose the truth and the triumph of any Christian relationship.

All those obstacles are strongly fortified. The Christian wife would do well to remember that "all have sinned and fallen short of the glory of God." This means that her spouse, just like she, is in process – learning to fight against sins that they were born with. If he is still yielding to some, she has strong spiritual weapons provided by God (prayer, fasting, kind words, etc.). She must not take his actions personally. It really is not about her. The sins of his heart are fortified by his long indulgences in sins and by the hold which these sins have on his soul. The wickedness of the world which God opposes is strongly fortified by the fact that the world emphasizes strong human passions; that one point strengthens another; that great numbers are united.

The idolatry of the world is strongly fortified by prejudice, and long establishment (always been done this way), and the protection of laws, and the power of the priesthood; and the opinions of the world are entrenched behind false philosophy and the power of subtle arguments. The whole world is fortified against Christianity, and therefore Christian relationships; and the nations of the earth have been engaged in little else than in raising and strengthening such strongholds for the space of 6,000 years.

The Christian wife goes forth against all the combined and concentrated powers of resistance of the whole world; and the warfare is to be waged against every strongly fortified place of error and of sin. These strong fortifications of error and of sin are to be battered down and laid in ruins by our spiritual weapons. She must never forget the availability of the wisdom of the Holy Spirit within her – the same Holy Spirit that hovered upon the water in Genesis chapter one and raised Jesus from the dead. She has nothing to fear but fear itself; for God is with her.

The Christian wife will always be challenged to choose whose methods to use, God's or the world's. The world would have her wear tightly fitting clothes, lots of make-up and adopt a way of speaking and acting that says "I don't need nobody; I am tough!" Ephesians 6:6 says "not by the way of eye service." Not those of the flesh. Not such as the people of the world use. They are not such as are employed by conquerors; neither are they such as people in general rely on to advance their cause. We do not depend on eloquence, or talent, or learning, or wealth, or beauty, or any of the external aids on which the people of this world rely. They are not such as deriving advantage from any power inherent in themselves. But our strength is derived from God alone. God's way is to concentrate on transformation from the inside out; our own; to acquire the fruit of the Spirit, which is love, joy peace, longsuffering, kindness, etc. If our faith in the Lord is genuine, it will usually prove itself over time at home, and in our relationships with those who know us best.

Paul assures us that God's mighty weapons - - Prayer, faith, hope, love, God's Word, the Holy Spirit – are powerful and effective. (See Ephesians 6:13-18). These weapons can break down the proud human arguments against God and the walls that Satan build to keep people from finding God or being able to get along with one another.

Understand Your Position is in Christ

"Not by might, nor by power, but by My Spirit, saith the LORD of hosts." Zechariah 4:6

My way led up a hill and right at the foot I saw a boy on a bicycle. He was pedaling up hill against the wind, and evidently found it a tremendously hard task. Just as he was working most strenuously and doing his best painfully, there came a trolley car going in the same direction – up a hill. It was not going too fast for the boy to get behind it, and with one hand to lay hold of the bar at the back. Then you know what happened? He went up the hill like a bird!

Then it flashed upon me! "Why, I am like that boy on the bicycle in my weariness and weakness. I am pedaling uphill against all kinds of opposition, and I am almost worn out with the tasks. Yelling at my spouse or trying to force my will on others is not working. But here at hand is a great available power, the strength of my LORD Jesus. I don't need to try to do it on my own.

"I have only but to get in touch with Him and to maintain communication with Him, though it may be only one little finger of faith, and that will be enough to cause His power to work all things together for my good and His glory for the doing of this bit of service that just now seems too much for me to handle." And I was helped to diminish my weariness and to realize this truth. The Holy Spirit is available to me if I will allow Him to lead me ….

Walk in Authority

1) **<u>Be dressed for a hostile environment</u>**. David was anointed before he went into hostile environments. (Commanding your morning through daily devotions and prayer before going out). Be sure you are a Christian; put on the whole armor of God before going to work, to school, or wherever. (**<u>John 16:33</u>** "I have told you

these things, so that in me you may have peace. In this world you will have trouble. But take heart! I have overcome the world.")

2) **Don't expect to be appreciated**. Appreciation is for relationships. As one of my Spiritual Fathers has said, "Get your appreciation and affirmations from home, your children, your spouse, your pet, your grandmother, etc. Expect from the job only what it has promised to give you – a paycheck. Don't come to a public place attempting to have personal relationships. Don't allow what you do to affect who you are." We can get tripped up expecting maturity from baby Christians. Age does not necessarily equal wisdom. (**Psalms 62:11-12** "One thing God has spoken, two things I have heard: "Power belongs to you, God, and with you, Lord, is unfailing love."; and, "You reward everyone according to what they have done.")

3) **Seek opportunities to change the atmosphere without commenting on the problems**. You can comment too much. What you say can trip you up. In quietness, confidence shall be your strength. Do your thing and let them talk about you (**Psalm 62:5-7** "Yes, my soul, find rest in God; my hope comes from him. Truly He is my rock and my salvation; He is my fortress, I will not be shaken. My salvation and my honor depend on God[,] He is my mighty rock, my refuge.")

4) **Do your job well, but remember your mission** (and authority comes from Christ). God put you there not to seek the light, but to be a light. (**Colossians 2:9-10** "For in Christ all the fullness of the Deity lives in bodily form, and in Christ you have been brought to fullness. He is the head over every power and authority.")

5) **Do not let your environment get inside of you**. You should influence it, not let it influence you. Stop going among people to be fed – you didn't come to receive, you came to give! (**Matthew 5:16** "In the same way, let your light shine before others, that they may see your good deeds and glorify your Father in heaven.")

6) **Increase your capacity to work with different personalities**. God will often bless you through people you don't even like if you respond in a godly manner. (**Philippians 2:3-8** "Do nothing out of selfish ambition or vain conceit. Rather, in humility value others above yourselves, not looking to your own interests but each of you to the interests of the others. In your relationships with one another, have the same mindset as Christ Jesus: Who, being in very nature[,] God, did not consider equality with God something to be used to his own advantage; rather, he made himself nothing by taking the very nature[,] of a servant, being made in human likeness. And being found in appearance as a man, he humbled Himself by becoming obedient to death— even death on a cross!")

7) **<u>Remember, where you are does not influence where you are going</u>**. Where you are is a temporary way-station on the way to where you are going. So are the people you are dealing with. This will deliver you from frustration. God (not the people), has a plan for your life. Keep your eye on the prize. When Peter did this, he was able to walk in what other people sank in. (**<u>Jeremiah 29:11,13</u>** "[11] For I know the plans I have for you," declares the LORD, "plans to prosper you and not to harm you, plans to give you hope and a future. [13] You will seek me and find me when you seek me with all your heart.")

8) **<u>Get the optimum results with minimum confusions</u>**. Be effective without making the environment worse. (<u>Proverbs 10:3-4</u> "The LORD does not let the righteous go hungry, but he thwarts the craving of the wicked. Lazy hands make for poverty, but diligent hands bring wealth.")

9) **<u>Don't be associated with one group or clique</u>**. Labels limit your usefulness. God wants you to work with everybody, but be labeled by no one. Use all your gifts (**<u>1 Corinthians 10:21</u>** "You cannot drink the cup of the Lord and the cup of demons too; you cannot have a part in both the Lord's table and the table of demons.")

10) **<u>Always keep your song near you</u>**. Keep a consecrated place in your soul. Hold on to your praise. So you will never have to *go to* God for help. He should be your stronghold at all times – going before you in the midst of trouble (**Psalms 34:1** "I will extol the LORD at all times; his praise will always be on my lips.")

CHAPTER XI

Pathways to Recovery: Finding Rest and Renewal

"But a Samaritan, as he traveled, came where the man was; and when he saw him, he took pity on him. He went to him and bandaged his wounds, pouring on oil and wine."
Luke 10:33–34

I want to encourage you with something that has the potential to change and bless your life like never before! God is the same, yesterday, today and forever. He wants to pour wine on your wounds and restore you not only to physical health, but also to emotional health and financial health. It's a truth from God's Word that comes to empower you when things get cloudy. God promises that you can live in perfect health and be fully restored. The fruit of the Spirit is peace, joy, love, kindness, longsuffering, faith, etc. Just walk in the Spirit, putting one foot in front of the other until you feel your strength returning.

Do Right When it Hurts

"The Lord will vindicate His people and will have compassion on His servants."
Deuteronomy 32:36

Commentary: Sometimes it is difficult, but you must force yourself to do the right thing, which is to turn every matter over to God. Sadly, the justice of God dictates that a person who has tried to hurt you may end up losing everything they have. That is not what we should pray for —or even rejoices in if it should happen, but remember that God's justice is always perfect. You should pray that God will turn this negative situation in your life for your good and His glory. Refuse to try to get even. Do not allow yourself to remain discouraged because of how someone else has treated you. With God's help, return good for evil and love in the face of oppression, hatred or indifference.

Get back to basics!

"Against You, You only, I have sinned and done what is evil in Your sight, So that You are justified when You speak and blameless when You judge. Behold, I was brought forth in iniquity, and in sin my mother conceived me. Behold, You desire truth in the innermost being, and in the hidden part You will make me know wisdom."
Psalm 51:4-6

Commentary: Sometimes God allows temptation in those areas of our lives that have not been surrendered to Him. Whatever has happened to you is a temptation from Satan. Now here's the key, Christians are not perfect, we will make mistakes; we will continue to be tempted to sin. But when we fall down, we must remember that we have an advocate in the Lord Jesus Christ, Who gives us the ability to get back up. You must at all times and in all circumstances be witnesses to the strength and power of God to forgive and restore. You must say, "No weapon formed against me shall perish." No one controls your destiny but God. He is bringing out truth in your innermost parts. God wants you wise to the schemes of the devil. He wants to shore up your walls so that the next thing down the road that tries to enter your life, you will recognize as not of Him. You will take appropriate steps to resist temptation and have it flee from you.

Get up and Stand!

"And we know that God causes all things to work together for good to those who love God, to those who are called according to His purpose." Romans 8:28

Commentary: If you keep on trusting God, He will bring you to a place of restoration and victory. Even though you may have gone through some bitter trials and you feel betrayed, deceived, let down, you must know that God is still with you. Sometimes God allows circumstances to happen to us because He wants to make a deposit into our life; open our eyes, make us more aware of what is going on all around us. He wants to toughen us up and make us more balanced for the ministry, but not have us cast down or become bitter. He wants to use us in a more excellent way to be a witness to others. In other words, God wants to use you to bless others. When adversity comes, let God have His way. Keep the faith. God wants you to be like that tree in Psalm one that is firmly planted by the rivers of waters. This tree has been bent by winds and storms, rains and snow. It has been tried and tested. You are like that tree. Say to yourself, "my restoration, my victory is on the way because I am an over comer. I will trust in the Lord because He cares for me and He is causing even this to work out for my good and His glory."

Keep Trusting God

"You will keep him in perfect peace all who trust in You, all whose thoughts are fixed on You." Isaiah 26:3

Commentary: All of us face disappointments from time to time. No matter how much faith you have or how good a person you are, sooner or later something or somebody will shake your faith to its very foundation. It may be something simple such as not getting that promotion you worked so hard for, not closing the big sale that you hoped for, not qualifying for a loan to buy that house you really wanted. Or it may be something more serious: A relationship falling apart, the death of a love interest or an incurable, debilitating illness. Whatever it is, that disappointment possesses the potential power to derail you and wreck your faith. That's why it's viable that you recognize in advance that disappointments will come and that you learn how to stay on track and deal with them when they do.

No matter what we have gone through No matter how unfair it was or how disappointed we were, we must release it and let it go. When you suffer loss, nobody expects you to be an impenetrable rock or an inaccessible island in the sea. It's natural to feel remorse or sorrow. But if you are still grieving and feeling sorrow over a disappointment that took place a year or more ago, something is wrong. You're hindering your future. You will have to rise up and say "I don't care how hard this is, I know God is with me and I am not going to let this get the best of me." Tell yourself that you know you cannot change a single thing about the past, but you can choose how you will live in the future.

Let God Be in Control!

"The LORD is my light and my salvation; Whom shall I fear? The LORD is the defense of my life; Whom shall I dread? ² When evildoers came upon me to devour my flesh, My adversaries and my enemies, they stumbled and fell. ³ Though a host encamp against me, My heart will not fear; Though war arise against me, In spite of this I shall be confident. ⁴ One thing I have asked from the LORD, that I shall seek: That I may dwell in the house of the LORD all the days of my life, To behold the beauty of the LORD And to meditate in His temple. ⁵ For in the day of trouble He will conceal me in His tabernacle; In the secret place of His tent He will hide me; He will lift me up on a rock. ⁶ And now my head will be lifted up above my enemies around me, And I will offer in His tent sacrifices with shouts of joy; I will) sing, yes, I will sing praises to the LORD. ⁷ Hear, O LORD, when I cry with my voice, And be gracious to me and answer me. ⁸ When You said, "Seek My face," my heart said to You, "Your face, O LORD, I shall seek." ⁹ Do not hide Your face from me, Do not turn Your servant away in anger; You have been my help; Do not abandon me nor forsake me, O God of my salvation! ¹⁰ For my father and my mother have forsaken me, But the LORD will take me up. ¹¹ Teach me Your way, O LORD, And lead me in a level path Because of my foes. ¹² Do not deliver me over to the desire of my adversaries, For false witnesses have risen against me, And such as breathe out violence. ¹³ I would have despaired unless I had believed that I would see the goodness of the LORD In the land of the living. ¹⁴ Wait for the LORD; Be strong and let your heart take courage; Yes, wait for the LORD." (Psalm 27)

Commentary: Did you know that God will cause you to remain? He will bring you to a place of stability and contentment. At one time, when adversity came, you would have gone backwards. You would have thrown your hands up in defeat and decided this place where I am is not for me. You would have tried to run away from gossip and cold stares; sought revenge by telling your side of the story. You would have been willing to change jobs, move to another state; change phone numbers, (whatever it took). You would have let your circumstances rule your choices.

But Jesus wants you to keep abiding in Him. He wants you to be like Paul who said that even though I am beat down, I will not let anything separate me from the God who loves me and sustains me. And in the process, you must know that God will take care of your enemy. You won't have to lift a finger in your own defense. Just pray to God about the circumstance and let God have at your enemy. God sees everything you've gone through; every sacrifice, every injustice. Payday is coming. He wants you to Get up and Stand! Don't talk about it; don't complain to anyone about it. I once had an older Lady, about 90 years old, who attended Bible Study with me for years. I can still see her sitting at the table the day she shared with us how she handles adversity. She would get on her knees and say, "Well God, what you trying to tell me this time?" We need to be like that old lady, know that God is in our good times as well as our adversities and say like the Psalmist, "I will wait for the Lord; I will be strong and let my heart take courage. Yes, I will wait for the Lord."

Tear Down the Walls!

"If you forgive others for their transgressions, your Heavenly Father will also forgive you.
But if you do not forgive others their transgressions, then your Heavenly Father will not
forgive your transgressions." Matthew 6:14-15

Commentary: When you forgive someone who has hurt or offended you, it's not simply about the other person; you're doing it for your own good as well. When you hold on to un-forgiveness and live with grudges in your heart, you are building walls of separation. You may think that you're protecting yourself, but you aren't. You are simply shutting other people out of your life. You become isolated, alone warped in prison by your own bitterness. Those walls aren't merely keeping people out, but those walls are keeping you pinned in. Do you realize that those walls will also prevent God's blessings from pouring into your life? They'll keep your dreams from coming to pass. You must tear down the walls. You must forgive the people who hurt you so you can get out of prison. You'll never be free until you do. Get that bitterness out of your life. You'll be amazed at what can happen when you release all that poison. Don't harbor any un-forgiveness in your heart. Ask God to shine the searchlight of the Holy Spirit on every nook and cranny of your being and let you see the areas where anything evil may be trying to gain a foothold through your own hesitancy to forgive. Pray and give the debt to God in Jesus' name.

My Prayer for you

"Heavenly Father, we live in a society that values competition, a dog-eat-dog world that encourages people to win at all costs. But that's not how you are at all. You are humble and kind and encourage us to love even our enemies. God, help us to love those who compete against us. Competition destroys relationship building. Help us to do the right thing and remember "Justice is mine; I will repay says the LORD." Help us to behave at all times with integrity and seek your "well done" blessing. Father help my reader to build her faith and believe that you will bring good even out of those circumstances she does not understand. Help her to hide Your Word in her heart that she might not sin against Thee. Close those doors that need to be closed and open those doors that need to be opened. I rebuke the enemy in her life and pull up by the roots any plan he has fashioned against her or her loved ones. I declare she is an Overcomer through the blood of Jesus the Christ. Help her to choose to trust You for good things in the days ahead. Remind her that You Oh God inhabit the praises of Your people. And even when things don't seem so good, remind her that all things are working together for her good and Your ultimate glory. Your eye is on the Sparrow so you are certainly watching over her. Teach her O God how to dance through the storms of life by seeking first the Kingdom and God and thereby gaining Your wisdom and Your strength to safely navigate through the trials of life. God, deliver her from the hateful pleasure of nursing a grudge. Instead remind her that she is following a lamb and help her choose to forgive. In the Name of Jesus. I declare it now, committing my reader and her situation into Your hands; and I step out on faith, counting it done, "Hallelujah!!!! Amen."

CHAPTER XII

Am I in a Toxic Relationship?

"I gain understanding from your precepts; therefore I hate every wrong path." Psalm 119:104

Can you feel intense affection for another and be realistic about their faults? Yes! Though it may be a rarity, it is possible. If you educate yourself as to the cause of your emotions, you can positively evaluate your love one for their good traits; and cover their faults (know they are not perfect but in process – as you are), and make an informed and balanced decision as to whether you can live with what you learn - or not. If you follow the teachings of the Bible, you can feel this way about everyone.

Feelings aren't facts. They are the results of the "good or evil" we attribute to things – our evaluations. But feelings can add to the enjoyment of life. As Paul discovered, if we think "right," we will only have appropriate emotions – we won't need to try to control them. (Philippians 4:8)

Warm feelings are nice feelings to have. But the harsh light of reality can cause them to wilt like an un-watered plant in the heat of the sun. The person that loves people because he understands God's plan, is probably the best choice for a lifetime companion. People that have something nice to say about everyone are much more willing to forgive and forget when they see us in the harsh light of day. They forgive the bad and accentuate the good. Romantic love has its place. Add to it mercy and kindness, and it is sheer beauty – a love journey that we can enjoy for the rest of our lives!

Relationship Quiz

Directions: Could you be in a toxic relationship and not even know it? This quiz is only intended to give you a " flavor" about the relationship you are in. The conclusions are self directed. It is generic enough to be used by either companion (male or female). It is also useful in either a long-term committed or budding relationships. Any "negative" answers should be meditated on very, very carefully before proceeding with the relationship. Just leave blank any questions that are not applicable, for example the section about children may not apply. Scoring Key is for each section of the quiz.

Scoring Key: 1 or more "negative" responses: signs of a troubled relationship; suggest discussing each "negative" with your significant other.
3 or more "negative" responses: signs of a unhealthy relationship, suggest you not proceed without counseling.

⭐Deal Breakers: Signs of physical or mental abuse are deal breakers because there is the serious possibility of life endangerment and should not be taken lightly. Seek counseling immediately; and be prepared to take their advice.

Accountability *Total Yes answers _____ Total No answers _____*

My significant other ignores worthy counsel from qualified mentors in their life? ___ Yes ___ No

The dominant others in my significant other's life are unworthy in my opinion? ___ Yes ___ No

My significant other has not impressed qualified mentors? ___ Yes ___ No

Do I admire and respect the mentors at whose feet my significant other sits? ___ Yes ___ No

Is my significant other addicted to any vice (Name it:_____) ? ___ Yes ___ No

Beauty *Total Yes answers _____ Total No answers _____*

Does my significant other criticize how I look? ___ Yes ___ No

Does my significant other constantly give me suggestions for improving my looks? Yes ___ No ___

Character *Total Yes answers* _____ *Total No answers* _____

Does my significant other laugh at things that should cause sadness? ___ Yes ___ No

Does my significant other show little pain or remorse concerning past mistakes and sins? ___ Yes ___ No

Has my significant other exited previous relationships peacefully? ___ Yes ___ No

Does my significant other break promises to me or to others easily and voluntarily? ___ Yes ___ no

Children **Total Yes answers** _____ *Total No answers* _____

Is my intended interested in either my children or having children with me? ___ Yes ___ No

Do I perceive my significant other as disobedient and arrogant? ___ Yes ___

Does my significant other put his children ahead of my concerns? ___ Yes ___ No

Does my intended attempt to divide me from the love and company of my children? ___ Yes ___ No

Does my significant other avoid criticizing the father of my children to them? ___ Yes ___ No

Communication *Total Yes answers* _____ *Total No answers* _____

Has conversation with my significant other become burdensome? ___ Yes ___ No

*Does my significant other give me advice that is contrary to the Word of God? ___ Yes ___ No

Does my significant other still understand and pleasure me? ___ Yes ___ No

Does my significant other communicate uncommon love through continuing to touch me, give me gifts, and spend time with me? ___ Yes ___ No

Is my significant other no longer willing to follow my personal advice or counsel? ___ Yes ___ No

Conduct *Total Yes answers* _____ *Total No answers* _____

Does my significant other show inconsistency in action and speech? ___ Yes ___ No

Does my significant other speak carelessly w/o considering the implications of what is being said? ___ Yes ___ No

Am I excited about introducing my significant other to those I care about? ___ Yes ___ No

Does my significant other enjoy the atmosphere of rebels? ___ Yes ___ No

Does my significant other become excited in the atmosphere of unbelievers, (able to relax, smile and talk easily)? ___ Yes ___ No

Does my significant other find breaking the law humorous and exciting? ___ Yes ___ No

Does my significant other keep confidences about hurtful or personal information involving others? ___ Yes ___ No

Does my significant other lie, use deception or exaggerate? ___ Yes ___ No

*Does my significant other use brute force (shoving, pushing or hitting) even in what they term horseplay? ___ Yes ___ No

★Cruelty *Total Yes answers* ____ *Total No answers* ____

Does my significant other call me unkind names when angry? ___ Yes ___ No

Does my significant other tease me excessively alone and/or in front of others? ___ Yes ___ No

Does my significant other like to horseplay or touch me in degrading ways? ___ Yes ___ No

Does my significant other take me for granted (sees no need to explain)? ___ Yes ___ No

Does my significant other tell me how to do things I am already quite capable of doing on my own? ___ Yes ___ No

Does my significant other continuously nag me to improve in certain areas? ___ Yes ___ No

Does my significant other boss me around as if I am a subordinate in the military? ___ Yes ___ No

Does my significant other continuously ignore my presence (moves/acts as though I am not around)? ___ Yes ___ No

Does my significant other make sarcastic/belittling remarks about me? ___ Yes ___ No

Does my significant other treat me harshly by yelling or advancing towards me in a menacing way when disapproving or angry with me? ___ Yes ___ No

Does my significant other correct me without reminding me that they love me? ___ Yes ___ No

Does my intended continue to reason with me/attempt to give me explanations when I am upset? ___ Yes ___ No

Does my significant other raise their voice when they get upset? ___ Yes ___ No

Does my significant other use foul language with or without getting upset? ___ Yes ___ No

Does my significant other show impatience, which may come across as rude? ___ Yes ___ No

Does my significant other say "no" without feeling that they need to give me a reason? ___ Yes ___ No

Does my significant other cut down things I am doing or planning (with or without asking for an explanation)? ___ Yes ___ No

Does my significant other cut down someone I spend time with? ___ Yes ___ No

Does my significant other spend the time to understand exactly what I am trying to say? ___ Yes ___ No

Does my significant other pout or stay angry when I've already conveyed that I know I was wrong ? ___ Yes ___ No

★Earning a Living *Total Yes answers* ____ *Total No answers* ____

Doe s my significant other refuse to find and keep a job? ___ Yes ___ No

Does my significant other use deception, cheating, illegalities, etc. to maintain job relationships? ___ Yes ___ No

*Emotional Stability *Total Yes answers ____ Total No answers ____*

Do pebble problems unleash mountains of anger in my significant other? ____ Yes ____ No

Does my significant other feel inferior to me, (does not feel confident, qualified or called of God to be my lifetime companion)? ____ Yes ____ No

Are there signs of addiction to drugs, alcohol, gambling or pornography in my significant other? ____ Yes ____ No

Are there signs of psychosomatic illness in my significant other, (frequent headaches, etc.)? ____ Yes ____ No

Family *Total Yes answers ____ Total No answers ____*

Does continuous strife exist between my significant other and their parents, or former caretakers? ____ Yes ____ No

Does my significant other's family hold contempt for me, and my assigned goals in life? ____ Yes ____ No

Does my significant other show interest in either my children or in having children with me? ____ Yes ____ No

Does my significant other have a good relationship with their own children? ____ Yes ____ No ____ NA

*Finances *Total Yes answers ____ Total No answers ____*

Can I trust my significant other to properly handle our finances? ____ Yes ____ No

Does my significant other constantly need a favor of money, etc.? ____ Yes ____ No

Goals *Total Yes answers ____ Total No answers ____*

Does my significant other make tactless comments about my projects or strivings? ____ Yes ____ No

Does my significant other notice my accomplishments? ____ Yes ____ No

Does my significant other make fun of my hopes, accomplishments and dreams? ____ Yes ____ No

Does my significant other make me feel I haven't tried to improve when I really have? ____ Yes ____ No

Does my significant other ask quality questions about my dreams or goals? ____ Yes ____ No

Does my significant other motivate me to a higher level of excellence? ____ Yes ____ No

Does my significant other criticize me unjustly? ____ Yes ____ No

Heart Treasures *Total Yes answers ____ Total No answers ____*

Does my significant other lack interest in things that are special to me? ____ Yes ____ No

Does my significant other give me the feeling that errors are not in their lifestyle? ____ Yes ____ No

Does my significant other pamper me when I don't feel well? ___ Yes ___ No

Does my significant other continuously dismiss my needs and wants in favor of their own needs & wants? ___ Yes ___ No

Does my significant other spontaneously hug me when arriving in my presence? ___ Yes ___ No

★Love *Total Yes answers* ___ *Total No answers* ___

Does my significant other have a relationship with God? ___ Yes ___ No

Is our relationship based on physical abilities and looks only? ___ Yes ___ No

Does my significant other fail to say "I love you", or show physical affection outside of sex? ___ Yes ___ No

Do I love truly myself? ___ Yes ___ No

If my significant other says "I love you," do I have trouble believing them? ___ Yes ___ No

Maintenance *Total Yes answers* ___ *Total No answers* ___

Is there continuous improvement in the relationship? ___ Yes ___ No

Does my significant other use deception, rebellion, stubbornness, etc. to maintain the relationship? ___ Yes ___ No

Is my significant other comfortable with rebellious, stubborn, arrogant, God-despising people? ___ Yes ___ No

Have I lost my desire to impress my significant other? ___ Yes ___ No

Does my significant other possess a passionate desire to give to me? ___ Yes ___ No

Are there nagging doubts about whether I will ever become the major focus in the relationship? ___ Yes ___ No

Opposite Sex, The *Total Yes answers* ___ *Total No answers* ___

Does my significant other feel a need for constant reassurance and attention from the opposite sex? ___ Yes ___ No

Does my significant other brag to me about past conquests? ___ Yes ___ No

Do I feel I cannot trust my significant other around my closest friends? ___ Yes ___ No

Does my significant other keep bringing up old mistakes from the past to deal with present problems? ___ Yes ___ No

Does my significant other fail to celebrate my presence in their life? ___ Yes ___ No

★Respect *Total Yes answers* ___ *Total No answers* ___

Does my significant other fail to show respect (say "thank you", excuse me," etc.)? ___ Yes ___ No

Does my significant other treat the favor of others with ingratitude? ___ Yes ___ No

Does my significant other show little respect for battles you've already won? ___ Yes ___ No

Does my significant other show little respect for the agenda and schedule of others? ___ Yes ___ No

Does my significant other make major decisions in life without pursuing my opinion? ___ Yes ___ No

Does my significant other continue to try to punish me after I've asked for forgiveness? ___ Yes ___ No

Does my significant other tell me verbally or by their actions that my opinions do not matter? ___ Yes ___ No

Does my significant other lack understanding at times when all I need is some support? ___ Yes ___ No

Spending Quality Time Together *Total Yes answers* ___

Does my significant other fail to spend quality time alone with me? ___ Yes ___ No

Does my significant other show inconsideration for me as a thinking, feeling human being? ___ Yes ___ No

Does my significant other show continuously that they are too busy to care or listen to me? ___ Yes ___ No

★Time in God's Presence *Total Yes answers* ___

Is my significant other willing to come before God in worship and prayer? ___ Yes ___ No

Am I in a big hurry to make a lifetime decision about marriage? ___ Yes ___ No

Where do I stand in this relationship? Do I feel secure? ___ Yes ___ No

Am I leaning on my own understanding instead of praying for an answer? ___ Yes ___ No

Am I sure this individual will make a worthy companion? ___ Yes ___ No

Trust *Total Yes answers* ___

Can I trust my significant other with my most painful memories? ___ Yes ___ No

Can I trust my significant other with my greatest fears or secrets? ___ Yes ___ No

Is my significant other quick to embrace an accusation against me? ___ Yes ___ No

Can I trust my significant other with the knowledge of my greatest weakness? ___ Yes ___ No

Do I feel that my significant other continuously builds me up and lets me down? ___ Yes ___ No

Do I feel that my significant other gets my hopes up but fails to follow through? ___ Yes ___ No

REFERENCES

Baltimore Catechism No. 4, Lesson 26 on Matrimony, Thomas L. Kinked

The Handbook of Bible Application, second edition, 2000 Neil S. Wilson, Editor

Life Application Notes

Meditations from *Streams in the Desert*

Merriam Webster's online Dictionary

The Message Bible or New King James Version

Pressing Past Anger and Unforgiveness, Joyce Myer

Raising Kids (The Dialog Series), 1993, Miller, Stephen M. Editor, Beacon Hill Press of
Kansas City

The Verbally Abusive Relationship: How to Recognize It and How to Respond, 1996,
Patricia Evans, Adams Media Corporation

Wikipedia online dictionary

Women are Spiritual BRIDGES, 2010, Bren Gandy-Wilson, Author House

Women of the Bible, 2003, Sue Poorman, Thomas Nelson, Inc.

Women of the Bible: The Life and Times of Every Woman in the Bible

Your Best Life Now, Joel Osteen

RESOURCE

<u>Help is available!</u>

Many services for troubled families are free or available at low cost. Check your local phone book for local listings.

- **Law enforcement agencies** can be called for intervention or protection.
- **Shelters offer emergency services**, such as short-term lodging, protection and counseling.
- **Family and social service agencies** provide counseling, protection, referrals and legal advice.
- **Legal aid offices** can provide legal help for victims who cannot afford a lawyer.
- **Hotlines** can provide immediate help for victims – and abusers. These include:

The National Domestic Violence Hotline at 1-800-799-SAFE (1-800-799-7233) or 1-800-787-3224 (TTY)

The **Childhelp National Child Abuse Hotlines** at 1-800-4-A-CHILD (1-800-422-4453).